OVERCOMING
WHEN YOU FEEL
OVERWHELMED

OVERCOMING
WHEN YOU FEEL
OVERWHELMED

5 STEPS TO SURVIVING THE CHAOS OF LIFE

JENTEZEN FRANKLIN

Chosen

a division of Baker Publishing Group
Minneapolis, Minnesota

© 2022 by Jentezen Franklin

Published by Chosen Books
11400 Hampshire Avenue South
Minneapolis, Minnesota 55438
www.chosenbooks.com

Chosen Books is a division of
Baker Publishing Group, Grand Rapids, Michigan

Printed in the United States of America

ISBN 978-0-8007-9983-0 (cloth)
ISBN 978-0-8007-9984-7 (trade paper)
ISBN 978-1-4934-3581-4 (ebook)

Library of Congress Control Number: 2021059283

Cover design by LOOK Design Studio

Author represented by The Fedd Agency, Inc.

Baker Publishing Group publications use paper produced from sustainable forestry practices and post-consumer waste whenever possible.

22 23 24 25 26 27 28   7 6 5 4 3 2 1

To all the volunteers who serve
within all our ministries
and outreaches at Free Chapel.

CONTENTS

Contents

ACKNOWLEDGMENTS

Special thanks to my very special friends Perry Stone Jr., Dr. Rich Rogers, Tracy Page, Jason Vernon, Laverne Bennett and Esther Fedorkevich for helping make this book possible. Your encouragement and input were a lifeline to this work. I love and appreciate you all very much.

Thank you to A. J. Gregory. It's always a joy to work with you. You're the best!

INTRODUCTION

Have you felt like giving up lately? I have. Our struggles may look different, but I'm sure you have endured a trying season in your life, as I have. Or maybe you are in the thick of one now. Maybe thoughts like these have constantly crossed your mind: *How did I get here? How can this be happening to our family?* You and I have different lives, but one thing we all have in common would be the overwhelming feelings that come from things like heartbreak, betrayal, addiction, mental illness, division, lies, deception, tears, sorrow, discouragement, fear, legal battles, shame, guilt, depression and the spiritual warfare we never even knew existed.

Are you sure you want to keep reading this book? I don't mean to trigger you, but it's only fair that I warn you—this book is not all about fairy tales and roses. It's a book about real life, real marriages, real families and a real Savior who loves us more than we can ever comprehend and who is still writing the script of our lives through every page of pain and confusion.

It feels as if our changing, challenging times have left a lot of people with a busted nest. That home, once a nice, cozy place to retreat to and rest in, has been dismantled piece by piece. God will sometimes allow our nest to be dismantled in order to teach us how to fly. What seems cruel can also be beneficial.

Many Christians have folded their wings and developed the nesting syndrome: a tendency toward stasis. The nest has become their security. But there comes a time when the momma eagle starts to disturb the nest so the eaglets can fulfill their potential (see Deuteronomy 32:11–12). What a nest of security could not do, a good stirring of the nest can. You are pregnant with promises. But mounting up with wings as eagles requires that you get out of the nest and into the air.

Is God disturbing your nest? You are not born to live and die in your nest. You are destined for higher ground. You have a heavenly calling.

Many churches have become nester churches, where comfort is valued above all else. But remember this: It's better to fail trying to fly than to sit in the nest and die. In Job 29:18, we find Job crying out. He says (paraphrasing), "I wish it were like the days of old. I wish I could go back to how it used to be, when everything was cozy and comfortable. For I said, *I will die in my nest.* But God said, *No, I didn't bless you to die in the nest. I'm going to take you higher than the rest of the birds can fly.*"

I relate to Job's cry. You may, too. Have you ever wondered how something so right—like a great relationship, a meaningful vocation, a spiritual calling, a God-designed dream—can turn out so wrong? The answer always is sin. It just creeps in through compromise, disobedience, rebellion, worldliness. Satan comes to steal, kill and destroy. And we're learning now, like never before, how to keep holding onto broken pieces until God makes some kind of sense of it all. The spiritual battle taking place now is real. The attacks you and I have gone through, and are likely still going through, are part of a much larger attack.

The end-time battle for the minds and hearts of our families is upon us. The battle for the mind is raging. Satan, the prince and the power of the air, is making an all-out attempt to seize this generation.

He is planting his thoughts of rebellion, lust, violence, drunkenness, depression, suicide, addiction and mayhem in the minds of millions. He is after our minds.

With the advancement of technology, Satan has issued new orders to corrupt the minds of this generation through the internet, movies, music and more. A constant diet of sensuality is being served. A barrage of evil thoughts assaults us daily. A deadly war between good and evil is raging. The battleground is not only in the heavens; it's also being waged between your ears. These are the days when Christians are being pressed upon from every angle.

Thankfully, God has left us His survival guide for the last days. We were warned in 2 Timothy 3:1 that "in the last days perilous times will come." The Greek word *chalepos*, translated here as "perilous times," is used twice in the New Testament—once in this verse, and once in Matthew 8:28, where it describes two demon-possessed men as being "extremely fierce." It is the same word in each verse.[1]

These are perilous, fierce times. Our world is facing moral crisis, spiritual crisis, social crisis, financial crisis and international crisis. It feels as though the world is going wild and nations are collapsing. To paraphrase Paul's description of the last days in 2 Timothy 3:2–5, "People will live for self alone. They will boast. They will be arrogant and proud and haughty, and children will be disobedient to parents. They will be *un*holy, *un*thankful, *un*loving and *un*forgiving." This is the Generation of *Un*s.

Don't let this discourage you. Things that seem out of our control are still in God's control.

God is in complete control, no matter what's going on in your life and in our world. You have not escaped His gaze. Because the world is not getting any better, because it's only getting worse, the Word of God must be where you and I focus our attention.

God wants you to be saturated with His Word and motivated by the Holy Spirit so you will be ready for the battle. He wants you to do more than survive these trying times. He wants you to thrive in these last days. So, how do we overcome when we feel overwhelmed, outnumbered, out-resourced and out of options?

If you're experiencing trouble, realize that the Lord Himself may be bringing you into the discipline of divine disturbance. All of us like it easy. We don't want any difficulty. We like the nest, don't we? But God has a purpose for disturbing our comfort and security. He wants us to discover our wings of faith. He wants us to know the joy of flying. God will often humble those He chooses to exalt. When God is going to use you greatly, there will be seasons where He'll allow you to hurt deeply.

> **God has a purpose for disturbing our comfort and security. He wants us to discover our wings of faith. He wants us to know the joy of flying.**

Your abasement is God's plan for advancement.

The Roman emperor Diocletian executed thousands of Christians, making sure they died in excruciating pain. He also banned the Bible by confiscating and burning as many as he could. Over the ashes of thousands of Bibles, he erected a monument that said in Latin, *Extincto nomine Christianorum*, which translated means "The name of Christians is now extinct." Twenty-five years later, the emperor Constantine declared the Bible to be God's Word. He remarked that it was infallible and that he would rule his entire kingdom by it. The Bible is the incorruptible Word of God. No matter how things seem, God's Word will prevail.

Before COVID, a lot of us were comfortably blessed. But God allowed our nests to be busted up. Job was familiar with that kind of scenario. He had a nice family, a successful business, good health, a blessed marriage. Then he lost it all. Satan did the busting up, but God allowed it. Through this turmoil, Job had to answer three questions—questions we also must face sooner or later:

14

1. *Can God be trusted when you're submerged in suffering?* Job lost his family, his finances, his physical health, even his reputation. But in the midst of the unimaginable loss, he learned how to praise God like never before. Faith is not about escaping suffering. Faith is enduring suffering through praise. Job made up his mind that he could trust God even when he was submerged in suffering.

2. *Can God be trusted when people you love forsake you?* Job wrote, "My relatives have failed, and my close friends have forgotten me" (Job 19:14). Have you ever been deeply hurt by close friends or family who said cruel things about you? Has your wife or husband abandoned you? Have your children cut you off? Has someone you trusted turned on you? Like Job, you must see that there is One who will never leave or forsake you. Especially when you're going through the darkest of days.

3. *Can you trust God when you're walking through extreme darkness?* Job was in absolute darkness. Are you there right now? He didn't have a clue what God was doing. Job thought God owed him some answers, but God never answered his questions. He just let Job keep walking in darkness. Can you trust God when He gives you no explanations and no light? God eventually did remind Job of His sovereignty, sufficiency and sympathy. And Job responded with praise. God restored Job double. And if you have the faith of Job, God will do the same for you.

In the midst of his trouble, heartbreak, misery, sorrow and difficulties, Job responded, "Though He slay me, yet will I trust Him" (Job 13:15). And if you'll trust God, as old Job did, God will prove Himself faithful, for all of heaven holds its breath in expectation of what your answer will be to this question of trust.

Even when you don't feel loved, God loves you. He is a personal God; He knows your name. And He is a purposeful God; He made you for a purpose. He is going to watch over and take care of you and your family. You are a chosen vessel for such a time as this.

If you've been feeling as if the battles you've been fighting the past few years have gotten a lot harder, there's a reason. Is the pull to click on that inappropriate website more powerful than ever? The urge to pick up what you've left behind stronger? The weight on your shoulders heavier? Does your heart race faster than you can remember? There's a reason.

Jesus is coming—and soon. But before that happens, the enemy's goal is to take out as many believers as he can. He aims to keep us from living the life God created us to live, and from telling others about the God who loves them and knows their name. The tormenting spirits of fear, discouragement, depression and lust are on high alert, zoned in on their target—you. The more the enemy can keep you distracted and dysfunctional, the less you will access your potential in the times God needs you the most—the last days.

When you read the words *end times*, what comes to mind? A nightmare? A fairy tale? Do you get overwhelmed and blank out? Or do you roll your eyes because you've heard this a hundred times before?

The Bible teaches that the end times should be a major part of our belief system. Unfortunately, for many it seems to be a scary, controversial, offensive or overwhelming topic. But the Church cannot stay silent about the end times any longer. If we ignore the truth about the Second Coming, we are teaching an incomplete gospel. We are also cheating ourselves and the next generation out of being prepared for the return of Christ.

Without understanding the full Gospel, life becomes about the here and now. Believers forget that they are responsible to witness to others about the free gift of salvation and the consequences for those who do not receive the Savior. And it's not always because we're selfish or trying to get ahead. Often, we forget because we are just overwhelmed!

We're so entrenched in the deadly traps of this world that the Second Coming of Jesus is the last thing on our mind. I mean, don't we have enough to deal with? Our focus is solely on survival. We're trying to make it through the day without reaching for a sniff or a sip, a click or a call, a binge or a spending spree, a panic attack or lethargy.

But God doesn't call us to survive. He calls us to overcome.

I wrote this book because deep in my spirit I sensed a lack of knowledge in the Church about the Second Coming of Jesus. I am also witnessing the spirit of Jezebel at work in the forms of lust, fear, discouragement and depression. Jesus Himself foretold the appearance of her legacy in Revelation 2, an idea I'll begin to explore in Part III of this book. Never before has there been such an epidemic of broken families and marriages, and of depressed Christians who feel overwhelmed just at the thought of going on.

God doesn't call us to survive. He calls us to overcome.

And yet, as Jesus told the ones who followed Him, do not be troubled. God has equipped you for this very moment.

The future is charged with enormous opportunity. We must look for Jesus daily and live as though He could come now. We must also occupy and allow God to use us, and to free us from the depression that rages, the addiction that whispers and the despair that seeks to eliminate our existence.

God has permitted you and me to live in this season of prophetic history. Let's strive to live well, no matter what the headlines, network news or social media outlets blare. Yes, there are giants out there. But remember that God has already given you what you need to fight them.

We're in a war. Some say it's a political war. Others say a cultural war or a war of ideas. More than all of those wars, we are in a spiritual war. And we can't win this war until we expose an enemy. What is really behind the abortion industry? The narcotic cartels? What drives the producers of porn? What motivates the sexual perversion and confusion that is so widespread in our nation and world? There is a mastermind behind it all: Satan himself.

Every generation before now has seen some of the signs of the end times come to pass. Yet we are the first generation forced to acknowledge that nearly every single end-time biblical prophecy has occurred, and that Jesus Christ could come at any minute.

We need to live as if we believe that. We need to live as if we have overcome, as if we are more than conquerors.

You may not be totally convinced that we are living in the last days. Maybe you're thinking, *But wait, Pastor Jentezen, I've already heard this before!* Did someone you know from a previous generation believe Jesus was coming in their time, but it didn't happen? In fact, don't many religious leaders try to convince us every year or decade or generation that this particular time is the end? Maybe you are drowning in a deluge of past warnings about the last days, without confirmation of prophetic truth.

My father, Pastor Billy Franklin, believed that Jesus was returning, and could return in his lifetime. I have been in ministry since I was a teenager and have always believed that the Lord was returning at some point, and that He might do so in my lifetime. With several generations before us believing that the Lord would return, why do I believe that the return of the Messiah is imminent?

Because we have crossed the Rubicon.

In ancient Rome, the Rubicon was a small waterway in northern Italy that marked the northernmost boundary of Rome proper. For a general to cross the boundary with his army meant an act of hostility—civil war, in fact. According to Roman law, crossing the

Rubicon was treason, punishable by death. In 49 BC Julius Caesar was a young general making a name for himself in what we now call France. In another part of the republic, General Pompey was acquiring territory in the east and south. Jealousy and strife divided these two leaders. When Caesar approached the Rubicon, he knew his options: Turn back and retreat, or cross and expect a fight. "Advance!" Caesar commanded his troops. "Let us go where the omens of the Gods and the crimes of our enemies summon us! The die is now cast!"[2] His crossing brought the onset of war and the death of Pompey, and it threatened the very existence of the Republic of Rome.

Today, the phrase "crossing the Rubicon" means to pass the point of no return. I believe this is where we are in the world today. We have crossed the line as it relates to prophecy, forging alignments and enacting laws that are contrary to the laws of God.

We crossed a Rubicon when prayer and the Bible were removed from public school. Our laws concerning legalized abortion are another example of crossing a Rubicon. Legalized abortion has been set in stone in America for 49 years. Abortion is not only legal up to 24 weeks of gestation (as in aborting a baby carried by a mother six months pregnant); some states have legalized it up until birth. We crossed a Rubicon when gay marriage was legalized and the White House was lit up with all the colors of the rainbow.

In this era of "cancel culture," what is right is called wrong, and what is evil is called good. Why don't we talk about this more? Why so secret? The cancel culture of silence hit the Church long before it engulfed the nation. It said, "Shut up about the Rapture. Shut up about end times. Shut up about heaven and hell. Shut up about it, because it's not in season and it hasn't been for over twenty years." A dangerous silence washed over the Church and its pastors, teachers and families.

There is great risk in preaching against the moral decline that is all around us today. Even in writing this book, I felt a pressure not to go on record saying something is wrong or immoral, knowing that this could be used as a headline to discredit me. But how can I not say what is true? I still dare to say that same-sex marriage is unbiblical. God still declares abortion to be the taking of an innocent life.

America has officially entered the "days of Lot," which is evident when you read Genesis 19. Because the signs of Christ's return are parallel to the days of Lot, these laws that have propelled us across the Rubicon may never be undone. Sadly, some of them are accepted and practiced even in some religious circles. When we look carefully at the original Greek words recorded in a statement Christ made, we find another interesting clue in connection with these national laws, this time in regard to the days of Noah. The verse reads: "For as in the days before the flood, they were eating and drinking, marrying and giving in marriage, until the day that Noah entered into the ark" (Matthew 24:38).

Why is marriage alluded to twice? To cover the wide variety of "marriages" seen in our day. In the verse it speaks of "marrying" and "giving in marriage." The word *marrying* here in Greek is *gameo*, which in general is a word used for marriage. Since this is a "days of Noah" sign, it could refer to marrying someone of either sex. The second phrase, "giving in marriage," refers more to a man who gives his daughter away to the man she is marrying. Since the fall of Adam and Eve in Eden, there has always been a sin nature within men and women, creating a clash between the flesh and the spirit. When we examine all the verses Christ spoke and the apostles recorded concerning what will unfold in the last days, however, clearly we are the first generation to see so many definite fulfillments.

We have now arrived at the acceleration of end-time events, many of which have been initiated in our generation and cannot be reversed!

While the world forecasts disaster, if you read the entirety of the end-times prophecy in the Bible, there's good news, great hope and a plan of escape for God's people. It all comes down to this simple question: "Whose report will you believe?"

In the last days, people will be starving for God's Word. But as believers, we refuse to participate in that famine. We're going to consume and believe God's Word over everything that we're going through. God said, "For he who sows to his flesh will of the flesh reap corruption, but he who sows to the Spirit will of the Spirit reap everlasting life" (Galatians 6:8).

Matthew 24:6–8 warns that in the end,

> You will hear of wars and rumors of wars. See that you are not troubled; for all these things must come to pass, but the end is not yet. For nation will rise against nation, and kingdom against kingdom. And there will be famines, pestilences, and earthquakes in various places. All these are the beginning of sorrows.

That's a bad report for sure. Then the very same chapter says, "And this gospel of the kingdom will be preached in all the world" (verse 14). That's an amazing report of revival! These two passages are in the same chapter, and both are 100 percent true. So we can focus on the good report, not just the bad report.

As a believer in Jesus Christ, I choose to focus on the good report. Think positively about the Father's blessings, goodness and faithfulness over your life. Always believe the report of the Lord. This is how we overcome in overwhelming times.

To help you overcome in these times, here is what you can expect from the rest of this book. In Part I, "Destined to Overcome," we will talk about how we are part of biblical prophecy and how, as we journey through life, there is a greater purpose at play. Then we will join Jesus and His disciples on a Temple tour that takes us through the words He spoke to them, and so also to us today, when He uncovered the signs of the last days (see Matthew 24). In that exchange, Jesus provided us with what I call 5 Steps to Overcoming through Overwhelming Times—steps that will help us face and rise above life's turmoil and troubles.

In Part II, "5 Steps for Overcomers," we will look more closely at the 5 Steps individually, which are *look within*, *look to Him* (Jesus), *look ahead*, *look out* and *look up*. Each step will not only help you and me overcome the chaos of the everyday, but will also enable us to embrace the mystery of the end times and encourage others to do the same.

Part III, "Get Up, Get Out, Get Free," takes us on a deep dive into the four characteristics of the end-time spirit that is attacking the Body of Christ today through its multiple manifestations of fear, discouragement, depression and lust. While the enemy desires to manipulate our minds, keep us captive to sin in our bodies and bring death to our spirits, God gives us the power to keep this from happening. My final chapter gives you an invitation to get up, get out and get free. New life can spring forth from addiction, anxiety, despair or whatever obstacles are overwhelming you in this moment. Freedom awaits.

Let's approach the last days not with chaotic living, fear or ignorance, but armed with knowledge and bursting with power because of Christ, who has already won!

Are you ready?

DESTINED TO OVERCOME

Have you ever been through a season in your life where you just can't understand it? Where you try tracing the line of your past to your present, but it doesn't seem to tell you anything about your future? Often, we forget that our life has an Author—a loving Father in heaven who chose to write our name into His story. And He wants to tell a fascinating story through our days . . . if we'll let Him.

In Part I, we're going to uncover the truth that while you're walking, God is working. God is over all, in charge, and you are on a prophetic journey toward His great purpose for your life. This is true, even when the chaos of life erupts and the signs of the last days flash before your eyes.

We will also take a little Temple tour with Jesus and hear His response to questions about what life will be like in the days leading up to His return. I will introduce you to 5 Steps I believe He gave us that will help you and me explore who we are in Him and how we live in these end times because of it. I want to show you how whatever overwhelms you might be the very thing that leads you to know Him better.

When You're Walking, God Is Working

Imagine that you are a basket maker who has been approached to make a special basket for a special purpose. You weave together papyrus reeds, overlapping one over another, then coat the basket with a double application of tar and pitch to prevent water from leaking through. You seal every crack with an artist's perfection. The basket is paid for and collected, and you never see it again. Years later, you discover how that very same piece of craftsmanship saved the life of an infant named Moses, marked by the Almighty to be Israel's greatest deliverer.

Imagine that you lived centuries ago in a town called Bethlehem. A clan of shepherds is concerned about the wild bears and lions that are attacking the flocks. The shepherds ask you for help in making them a crude weapon, something small enough to carry yet strong enough to defeat these predators. You fasten a piece of woven wool between two strips of leather and admire your finished product. Your name will never be spoken of as the creator of this weapon, but this slingshot will go down in history, made famous by a teenage warrior named David when he used it to slay Goliath.

Over a thousand years later, in the same city, imagine you are the owner of a village inn. A major tax has been imposed, and every family must return to the family's birthplace to register for a census. You hear a knock on the door. Before you stands a man, along with his pregnant wife sitting on a donkey. She is ready to go into labor at any time. They ask for a room, but you have none available. You offer them all you have left, a stable where you keep the animals. You are unaware that you have just provided the birthplace where the Messiah of the world will be born. Your stable will be celebrated every year when the world remembers the birth of the infant Christ.

What would it be like to participate in an event that was predicted in the Bible thousands of years ago? You might not even fully realize it in the moment. As far as you're concerned, you're just doing something you always do. Or, you might feel helpless and hopeless, and yet one act of obedience can spark the outburst of an ordained journey. Would you recognize God at work in a divine moment as you walk it out?

You Are on a Prophetic Journey

You are part of biblical prophecy at this very moment. Our generation has been marked with prophetic promises. God is allowing us to see events unfolding that the ancient prophets only saw in visions and dreams.

It's easy to forget that God is orchestrating behind the scenes as we go about our business in the process of living our lives. He has sent you on a prophetic journey. If you trust Him, you can know that He is in control and that He holds you in His hand.

Read that last line again. Does it comfort you or frighten you? You are reading this book for a reason. You can't take another sleepless night. You can't kick a habit that has morphed into a full-blown addiction that is destroying your relationships with those around you.

Food is more than a comfort; it is a source of security, yet it never satisfies that hunger that growls deeper each passing day.

Take a breath. Deeply, this time. Your story can change, right now.

One encounter, an inconvenient detour, even the desperation of wanting to heal from a trauma, can bring you one step closer to where God wants you to be—whole and healed, filled with joy and purpose, ready and able to carry out whatever mission He has planned for your life. He is always at work, even if you've numbed yourself to the point that you can't even see it anymore.

God is still working it out while you are walking it out. And if you are available and willing, He can give you the tools you need to overcome the nightmares that are plaguing you and keeping you from the ultimate destiny He has prepared for you.

I think of Saul before he even knew he would become the first king of Israel. At the time, he was a young man living in his father's house, gulping down a bowl of cereal when his dad tasked him with a mission. The dad didn't tell the son to take out the trash or pick up some toilet paper. He told Saul that three donkeys were missing and that it was Saul's job to find them.

"Please take one of the servants with you, and arise, go and look for the donkeys," Saul's father said (1 Samuel 9:3). The Bible doesn't tell us what the relationship was like between father and son, but if Saul was a typical teenager, he probably rolled his eyes and groaned in response. You know, just because his father told him to do something.

Saul had no idea at that point of the destiny God had for his life. He had no clue that the mission his father was sending him on would culminate in his being anointed the first king of Israel. He didn't know that he was on the brink of beginning a prophetic journey for a whole nation that would produce a Messiah. And that one day, this Messiah would come back and that His Kingdom would never end.

Saul just thought he was doing what he had to do, obeying his annoying father and doing another dumb chore. So he and a servant went on a journey, which lasted three days, to look for the missing donkeys. The men searched the land for these braying animals and could not find them. Saul was ready to give up. He told his companion, "Come, let us return, lest my father cease caring about the donkeys and become worried about us" (1 Samuel 9:5).

But the servant had a better idea: "'Look now, there is in this city a man of God, and he is an honorable man; all that he says surely comes to pass. So let us go there; perhaps he can show us the way that we should go. . . . Come, let us go to the seer'; for he who is now called a prophet was formerly called a seer" (verses 6, 9).

While Saul was moving in one direction, God was also moving in another; He had already spoken to the prophet about the young man's arrival. I love the fact that God was working on both sides. He was setting up the right situation, the right person, the right place and the right time. And when God was ready . . . a collision of destiny.

This is what it means to be on a prophetic journey. It happened to Saul. It happened to the basket weaver, the slingshot maker and the innkeeper. And right now, it's happening to you. It's time to root out what has been holding you hostage from God's plan.

The day before Saul and the servant decided to seek out the prophet/seer, Samuel, God had told the prophet,

> Tomorrow about this time I will send you a man from the land of Benjamin, and you shall anoint him commander over My people Israel, that he may save My people from the hand of the Philistines; for I have looked upon My people, because their cry has come to Me.
>
> 1 Samuel 9:16

The Bible says that the Lord "told Samuel in his ear" about Saul coming (verse 15). This is so powerful. We can't speak if we don't hear. We need a sensitive ear, like the prophet. We need to listen for God's words.

While Saul and his servant were on their way to the city to look for the prophet, Samuel was walking toward them from the opposite direction:

> So when Samuel saw Saul, the LORD said to him, "There he is, the man of whom I spoke to you. This one shall reign over My people." Then Saul drew near to Samuel in the gate, and said, "Please tell me, where is the seer's house?"
>
> Verses 17–18

And suddenly, the paths of two men, strangers to one another, on journeys of their own and with separate agendas, hurtled into one another with power enough to unlock the prophecy of a future King with an eternal Kingdom.

Samuel answered Saul and told him,

> I am the seer. Go up before me to the high place, for you shall eat with me today; and tomorrow I will let you go and will tell you all that is in your heart.
>
> Verse 19

And before Saul could get a word in, Samuel added (in paraphrase), "Oh yeah, and those donkeys you're looking for? Don't worry about them. They're found and taken care of, waiting for you to take them back home."

You may not see it or even believe it yet, but you are on a prophetic journey.

The three men broke bread. Saul and his servant spent the night at the prophet's house. The next day, Samuel made Saul send the servant back home ahead of him, and then began to prophesy over and anoint Saul as the first king of Israel.

You may not see it or even believe it yet, but you are on a prophetic journey. Sometimes, it takes losing donkeys to discover what God's plan was all along.

Looking for Donkeys, Finding the Kingdom

God orders our steps. We might think we're doing one thing, but there's a purpose underneath what we see on the surface. What you are going through right now—the depression, the grief, the discouragement, the disappointment, the sexual addiction, what the enemy is trying to use to destroy you—can be the very thing God will use to lead you where you are supposed to be.

In Saul's case, God used a loss in his life to shift him in a prophetic direction where he would encounter a prophet who would forever change his life, and the word of the Lord would then be actualized. This young man went out looking for donkeys and came back home with the kingdom.

Something was missing in Saul's life. Are you in a season where something is missing? Have you recently lost something? Has your marriage just ended? Have you said good-bye to a loved one? Has a dream that you longed for and worked tirelessly for been rerouted in a different direction? Sometimes, what is missing in our lives is the very reason we find God's plan for our lives.

God can use what we've lost to get us back on our prophetic journey. Saul was chasing donkeys, in his mind a trivial and unimportant assignment compared to the magnitude of his calling. You may be on your third kind of medication to help stabilize your moods. You may be defeated by the number of starts and stops you've had on your journey to recovery. Many times, the challenges of this life are actually a setup for God's next assignment for you. God can use what you don't have and what you're looking for—like peace, joy or meaning—to return you to your destiny or even to help you discover it.

You may think you're chasing donkeys, but you're about to come home with the Kingdom. The prophet told Saul, in effect, "It's time to stop chasing donkeys! They're just distractions!" God had something much bigger for Saul than chasing donkeys. Saul would be king.

We can miss what God has for us because we're chasing what's unimportant. The enemy wants to keep us feeling anxious, keep us occupied with distractions, paralyze us with confusing messages and render us helpless. But God has placed us here for such a time as this.

It's time for you to stop chasing donkeys.

I believe the Lord has a word for you if you are reading this book. I believe He wants you to know that He has already taken care of the issues of your life. You may have no idea how God is about to use you, but you can be sure that the enemy wants to limit you. God has amazing things planned for you. Don't make the mistake of getting caught up chasing donkeys when you are headed for the throne. You are a king or a queen in the Kingdom of God.

God is setting appointments, opening doors and arranging finances for you and your near future. God is about to take you into your most productive season, if you'll stop chasing donkeys and stop hiding in your own insecurity.

After Samuel anointed Saul and declared he would be king, the big day came. All of Israel gathered by the tens of thousands to crown Saul as their first king. It was a huge celebration. The men were celebrating in the streets; the women were dancing with timbrels and tambourines; the children had streamers in their hands. There was one problem—Saul was nowhere to be found.

> **God is about to take you into your most productive season, if you'll stop chasing donkeys and stop hiding in your own insecurity.**

Where was their king? They announced his name again, but still he did not come forth: "Therefore they inquired of the LORD further, 'Has the man come here yet?' And the LORD answered, 'There he is, hidden among the equipment'" (1 Samuel 10:22). The word *equipment* here was originally the term for baggage. Saul was so insecure that he could not step into what God was calling him to do. Instead, he went and hid in a pile of baggage.

Like Saul, we will miss what God has for us if we aren't willing to let go of our baggage. This is one of the ways the enemy will try to keep you from receiving the blessings of God. You have to stop chasing donkeys that don't really matter in the big picture of God's plan, because that kind of baggage from the past will hold you back from your calling. (You'll read in Part III about some of the baggage that can hold us back. And when you get there, you'll learn there is a better way.)

It's not about your strength or your ability; it's about trusting God. And before you can even begin to roll your eyes or interrupt me with a "But, Pastor," you should know that God doesn't accept excuses when we are on a prophetic journey.

The One, the Place, the Time

You are the one. *This* is the place. *Now* is the time.

When faced with God's calling, however, I find that most people hide behind a multitude of excuses about why they are not the man or woman for the job: *I can't because . . .*

I'm too young.
I'm too old.
I don't know what I'm doing.
I'm not worthy.
I can't get clean.
I can't get out of debt.
I can't stop struggling with depression/anxiety.

When Samuel first began to prophesy over Saul, the young man refused to accept his destiny. Saul made excuses: "Am I not a Benjamite, of the smallest of the tribes of Israel, and my family the least of all the families of the tribe of Benjamin? Why then do you speak like this to me?" (1 Samuel 9:21). *I'm the least of the least from the most dysfunctional family in town.* But God knew what He was doing then, and He knows what He is doing today.

Your excuses are what God wants to use! He will take your excuses and make them opportunities. God has a purpose for your life, filled with assignments that require your unique DNA.

I want you to get three truths into your heart today. Make these a personal revelation:

1. You are the one.
2. This is the place.
3. Now is the time.

Scripture is replete with people whom God came to with a magnificent plan for their life. And yet, their responses were the same: *Not me.* Take Moses, for instance. When God spoke to him through a burning bush, the man's response was a list of excuses: *I'm slow of speech. No one will listen to me.* The same thing happened with Gideon. The angel of the Lord approached Gideon and, before tasking him with an assignment, called him a mighty man of valor. Gideon's reply? *You have the wrong guy. I'm the least of the least.*

These are just two of a plethora of characters in the Bible who said, *I'm not the one. This is not the place. Now is not the time.* God had to turn the situation around so these people could understand that they were the one, that was the place, and it was the right time.

On January 13, 1982, Air Florida Flight 90 crashed into the 14th Street Bridge seconds after takeoff from Washington National Airport. The plane landed in the frozen Potomac River. Out of 79 people aboard, only 5 survived. Lenny Skutnik, a federal employee, stood nearby. A bystander in a crowd of hundreds of others, when he heard the screams of passengers trying to survive in the icy water as rescue efforts were underway, he tore off his coat and dove into the frigid river. He was able to save a woman and bring her safely to the riverbank.

And Skutnik didn't know it, but according to one report there was a woman in her apartment who was watching the live newscast, and she turned to her two little children and said, "That looks like something your father would do." She found out three hours later that it was indeed their father, her husband! Are you the one? Are you the person who will stand up and say, "I am the one to do something about this. This is the place, and now is the time"?

Alfred Nobel is known to us today as the scientist who established the Nobel Peace Prize to recognize people's achievements in physics, chemistry, physiology, medicine and literature, or for their work toward peace between the nations. But according to historian Oscar J. Falnes, Nobel's family name was once "associated not with the arts of peace but with the arts of war."[1]

Though Nobel never told this story publicly, historians suggest that his benevolent motivation sprang up from an error in the local paper. One day, Alfred was reading a French newspaper and stumbled upon a scathing obituary about . . . himself! In this obituary, Alfred was labeled as a "merchant of death."[2] Known for inventing and developing explosives (including dynamite) used in both construction and warfare, Alfred was horrified at the legacy he had supposedly left. While the newspaper's error of mistaken identity was corrected—the paper had meant to identify Alfred's brother, Ludwig, who had died—Alfred had an awakening of sorts. According to biographer Kenne Fant, Alfred "became so obsessed with his posthumous reputation that he rewrote his last will, bequeathing most of his fortune to a cause upon which no future obituary writer would be able to cast aspersions."[3] Nobody today thinks of Alfred

Nobel as the inventor of explosives. We think of him as a man who advanced peace through the Nobel Peace Prize.

You can redetermine your legacy. You can't redo what you've done, but you can turn yourself around, starting now, and live a life that counts for the Kingdom. I want the same spirit that gripped Alfred Nobel to grip you and me—*I am the one. This is the place. Now is the time.*

It's so easy to think that God is going to do something in distant places or at another time in our life, but the Bible tells us that today is the day of salvation (see 2 Corinthians 6:2). And this is the place!

When Moses and the people of Israel were wandering in the wilderness, in one of many instances the people started to whine and complain: "We're dying of thirst!" "We're starving!" "There's nothing to eat or drink!" "We're tired!" "It's hot!" (See Numbers 21:4–5.) Plenty of them were thinking, *This is ridiculous. Why on earth did we listen to Moses and leave Egypt? Let's go back.*

But God said, "This is the place." And in the middle of the wilderness, without food and without drink for the people, God told Moses to stay. More than that, He told him to do something else: "Get out the Levitical choir, Moses. It's time to start singing!"

Here's how I imagine this pathetic scene. These people are out in the desert. Dust everywhere. Hot as fire. They have been on the move for a while and are weary. But the choir gets up and starts singing:

Spring up, O well!—Sing to it!—the well that the princes made, that the nobles of the people dug, with the scepter and with their staffs.

Numbers 21:17–18 ESV

And as they sing, the priests start tapping the dry dirt with their staffs. *Tap. Tap. Tap.* All they are doing, it seems, is creating a cloud of dust. Some start coughing. Others start choking. But they continue to pound the earth, and the choir continues to sing. I can imagine one of the priests pounding his staff into the ground, but this time it gets stuck. He can't pull it out of the ground, so he calls Moses over. Both of them grasp the staff with all their might and jerk that rod out of the ground. But wait—the end of the stick is dripping wet. Moses says, "Hit it again!" And with the background of "Spring up, O well!" water starts gushing out of the dry ground.

Stop thinking that God is only going to use you after you get married, when you find the perfect job, once you move to the perfect city, after the fighting stops in your family or once you're finally over that temptation. Start saying, "I am the one. This is the place. Now is the time."

The author of Ecclesiastes wrote that a living dog is better than a dead lion (see Ecclesiastes 9:4). As powerful as a lion is, if he's dead, his power is nothing more than a lost opportunity. For him, it's over. I do not want to be a dead lion. I would rather be a living dog. As small a dog as I may be, if I'm breathing, there is still life ahead. I still have a chance.

A present opportunity plagued with problems is better than an awesome opportunity that has passed. Now is the time! The people of Israel refused to march into the Promised Land because they listened to the ten spies. Moses tried to intervene for them and asked God to pardon them, but God basically answered, "You're too late. I'm not going to use you. I've already chosen another generation to enter the Promised Land" (see Numbers 14:18–23).

Again, now is the time! Did you know that if you wait until it's too late, you can miss your destiny? You can miss your purpose? You can miss the plan God has for your life? "Now is the time. Today is the day." When are we going to quit saying, "One day, we're going to do something; one day, we're going to make a difference; one day, we're going to really win the world; one day, we're going to change our nation; one day, we're going to influence this country for God"? And when are we going to say "Now is the time"?

This is the moment! This is the place! There will never be a greater time to give your best, to give your all, to pour your life out on God, than right now.

You are the one. This is the place. Now is the time.

Awaken to your destiny today. You were created to be the salt and the light of the earth. You can't do anything about your past, but you can rewrite the rest of your life. It starts right now.

What are you waiting for?

The Temple Tour and the 5 Steps

For thousands of years, people have speculated about the last days and the return of Jesus. The disciples were no different. Matthew 24 recounts one of the most important prophecies in the Bible. In that Scripture, we read how during the last week of Jesus' life, the disciples went with Him to the Temple, the crowning achievement of the Jewish people. As they strolled through the architectural magnificence, gaping in awe at all its splendor, the disciples somehow forgot that Jesus was the carrier of the presence of God, a presence that had vacated that Temple.

The disciples thought Jesus would be as impressed as they were at what men had done to build the Kingdom of God, but Jesus was not at all impressed by what mankind could do. He said something that caught them off guard: "Do you not see all these things? Assuredly, I say to you, not one stone shall be left here upon another, that shall not be thrown down" (Matthew 24:2).

This comment messed them up. Fast-forward 24 hours, and Jesus and the disciples were at the Mount of Olives across the valley, looking down on that same Temple. Contemplating the words Jesus had spoken the previous day about the Temple, they gathered to ask Him, "When will these things be? And what will be the sign of Your coming, and of the end of the age?" (verse 3). And Jesus, in His unique way, didn't answer the question they were asking. Instead, He gave them the answer they would need: "Take heed that no one deceives you" (verse 4).

The phrase *take heed* is translated in various versions as "be careful" (AMP), "see to it" (NASB) and "watch out" (CJB). Four times in Matthew 24, Christ warned of being "deceived" (see verses 4, 5, 11, 24). To deceive someone refers to seducing that person and causing him or her to wander out of the right path.

Jesus didn't load the disciples down with the many signs of the times, nor did He tell them when He was going to come. They didn't need the exact time and every sign. What they needed most was simply to "take heed" to themselves. In other words, make sure they were on their toes. Make sure they were making the right, godly choices.

The same is true for us today. When responding to these "return of Christ" kinds of questions, Jesus said then what He is saying to believers all over the world today: *What you know or don't know about the end times isn't nearly as important as who you are when I return.* He also gave us "5 Steps" we can take that will help us explore who we are as we approach the end times. We will look at each of these steps more closely in Part II ahead, but here they are together in a list:

> Jesus said then what He is saying to believers all over the world today: What you know or don't know about the end times isn't nearly as important as who you are when I return.

- Step #1 *Look Within*
  - "Take heed that no one deceives you" (Matthew 24:4).

- Step #2 *Look to Him*
  - "See that you are not troubled" (verse 6).

- Step #3 *Look Ahead*
  - "He who endures to the end shall be saved" (verse 13).

- Step #4 *Look Out*
  - "This gospel of the kingdom will be preached" (verse 14).

- Step #5 *Look Up*
  - "Now when these things begin to happen, look up and lift up your heads, because your redemption draws near" (Luke 21:28).

I love how Jesus shifted gears in Matthew 24. It's almost as though He did it on purpose. I'm sure by now He was used to people asking Him about the latest prophecy to satiate their curiosity, or begging Him for a sign to bolster their faith. But Jesus knew what was most important—preparing His followers spiritually, emotionally and mentally for what was to come.

We may be living in perilous times, but they are also times filled with tremendous opportunity. Don't be filled with worry. Be strong and courageous because we serve the God of hope.

Old Weapons, New Victories

Sometimes it takes an old sword to slay new giants.

After David is anointed as the future king of Israel, he levels up. Instead of fighting lions and bears, he finds himself in the ring with a nine-foot warrior named Goliath. You probably know the story. This teenage runt, overlooked by his father and brothers, grips a bag full of five smooth stones and steps onto a bloodied battlefield. Goliath mocks the poor kid, but David is anything but afraid.

"When this is over," he tells the giant, "I'm going home. You, however, are going down."

One stone, one shot and the insulting warrior is dead. David seals the deal by decapitating Goliath with the fallen giant's own sword. Cue the celebration—the teenage boy is hailed as a hero and invited to live in the palace with King Saul. He has to be thinking that his time to reign is quickly approaching.

Fast-forward many years. David still is not on the throne. Instead, he is being chased out of the palace by the jealous king. David finds himself running for his life, a season that stretches into many years. He is an unprepared fugitive. No plan, no money, no weapons, no extra clothes, no canned goods, no GPS.

Where does he run to first? The Temple. I love that. In his darkest day, he chooses to run to the Temple. Not to a bar. Not into the arms of a woman. Not into the clutch of an addiction. But to the place where the presence of God is found (see 1 Samuel 21). Where do you run when you're in trouble?

In the Temple, David meets a priest by the name of Ahimelech. The fugitive asks for food, and the priest gives him bread and probably some wine. As David stuffs his mouth, crumbs sticking to his beard and collecting on his cloak, he asks Ahimelech for one more thing: "Um, I know this is an unusual request, but I was in such a hurry that I left without my weapons, and I might need some out here. Do you have any weapons in the house of God?"

The priest shakes his head. "No, we're preachers here, not fighters."

> In his darkest day, David chooses to run to the Temple . . . to the place where the presence of God is found. Where do you run when you're in trouble?

Before disappointment can shadow David's heart, Ahimelech's face lights up. "Wait a minute. As a matter of fact, we have one weapon. It just so happens that we have the same sword you used to cut off Goliath's head! Would you like that one?"

The same sword for a new victory? It may have been old, but it was just as sharp. And if it had worked then, surely it would work now.

Can you imagine David's eyes when the priest showed him the weapon once brandished by the very giant who had threatened to kill him? In a split second the young man was surely transported back to that battlefield, the triumphal chanting of thousands ringing in his ear. The boy had brought the sword to the Temple because he knew the One to whom the victory belonged.

Back in the Temple, older and on the run, facing a new fight and a different enemy, David reaches for the same glistening instrument of war. The sword is even more than he was looking for; it is just what he needs. So I can imagine the future king whispering in awe to the priest, "There is none like it; give it to me" (1 Samuel 21:9).

The weapons God provided for us in the past still work today. The same name that is above all names, the same blood that was shed on the cross, the same power of the Holy Spirit, the same tools of praying and fasting—these are not meant for us to showcase in church as props, but to use as weapons to endure and thrive, particularly in these end times.

Think of these 5 Steps—*look within, look to Him, look ahead, look out* and *look up*—as weapons you can use to overcome, no matter what life throws your way.

PART II

5 STEPS FOR OVERCOMERS

Seasons of struggle call for spiritual support. Jesus told us that in this world we would find trouble. He also offered us ways to overcome those troubled times we would face.

In this part of the book, we will look at 5 Steps that are instrumental to overcoming in overwhelming times. They teach us to *look within*, *look to Him*, *look ahead*, *look out* and *look up*. Coming straight from the words of Jesus, they will help us face both our everyday challenges and the unique end-times challenges we now see arising.

Using these 5 Steps, we can explore our understanding of who we are in Christ and how we live because of Him. Each of these steps will encourage us to get up, get out and break free.

Step #1: Look Within

The enemy sees you as a high-value target, or HVT. The United States Department of Defense defines this military term as "a target the enemy commander requires for the successful completion of the mission. The loss of high-value targets would be expected to seriously degrade important enemy functions throughout the friendly commander's area of interest."[1] So an HVT describes an enemy combatant who has the potential to do great damage or create a disruption to operations. Before his capture in 2003, former Iraqi president Saddam Hussein was known as "High-Value Target Number One" by the United States military. Osama bin Laden was another such HVT.

The more you know about God, the more you love and serve Him, the more you abide in His Word, the more you become a high-value target, or HVT, of the enemy. Guaranteed. And when you're guaranteed to make hell's most wanted list, you're going to need strategic survival and overcoming tactics.

As a believer living in the end times, you are a threat. The enemy knows that God has given you the keys to the Kingdom. If you know how to pray, how to fast, how to walk in the Spirit, how to love and forgive, you're an HVT, and hell is sending its best forces to eliminate you from this world. This may frighten you, but it is actually good news. It is evidence that you are an asset to the Kingdom.

Simon Peter was one of many HVTs in the Bible. In Luke 22, we find Jesus sitting at a table with His disciples at the Last Supper. As the evening draws to a close, Jesus turns to Peter, and calling him by his original name, says, "Simon, Simon! Indeed, Satan has asked for you, that he may sift you as wheat" (verse 31). Some translations use the word *separate* instead of *sift*, meaning Satan's desire is to separate this disciple from Jesus, as one would separate wheat from husks.

What does this mean to you and me today? The enemy's goal is to sift us, too, which means he wants to separate us. He wants to sift you from your godly friends, colleagues and family members. He wants to cause division in your marriage. He wants to breed conflict in your friendships. He wants to bring about contention in your relationships with your children. He wants to separate you from the right crowd and connect you to the wrong one. Hell is trying to pull you away from what God has destined for you, and the enemy doesn't care what it costs.

Take Heed

As we saw in chapter 2, the first thing Jesus told His disciples when they asked Him to tell them the signs of the last days was, "Take heed that no one deceives you" (Matthew 24:4). Instead of giving His followers a timeline, He told them to *look within*—our first step to overcoming. In other words, they needed to self-reflect and guard themselves. It's not so much about knowing the why, where, when or how; what matters is what's happening within you.

Again, as I said in chapter 2, Jesus was telling them the same thing He is saying to believers all over the world today: What we know or don't know about the end times isn't nearly as important as who we are when He returns. How is your thought life? What is the condition of your character? How is your integrity? Personal holiness may not be the most thrilling of topics to discuss, but "take heed"—it's one of the most important battles you and I will fight.

Many of our spiritual battles are born of self-inflicted wounds. We fall into routines that hinder our growth. We invest our time battling on keyboards behind screens instead of praying for one another. We check 24-hour news feeds because we are obsessed with trying to figure out what's happening in another part of the world. We try to connect the dots of our world with end-time prophecy in the Bible, while our neighbor might not even know that we love Jesus.

Here's a simple question: How do we make looking within a priority?

When you compare the amount of time you listened to podcasts or scrolled through social media last week to the time you spent in God's Word, which wins? Don't get so busy with entertainment, politics, personal finances and problems that you lose track of the one thing God told you to guard—yourself. Be on your toes. Make godly choices.

Your goal is to endure to the end and overcome in the areas in which you struggle. Know that what I like to call *weapons of mass distraction* will be thrown in your path to stop your forward momentum. Don't fall for them. Stay on guard. Look within.

Take heed.

Guard Yourself

The number one responsibility of every man and woman to look within is found in an Old Testament story that takes place on a battlefield. As you can imagine, a battlefield breeds continuous chaos. In Old Testament times, the battlefield was full of blaring horns, clashing swords, the thunder of rumbling chariots, bellowing battle cries and the moans of dying soldiers. Every minute was crucial. Every action, every decision counted. Lives were at stake then.

Now, in the spiritual battle you wage, your life is still at stake. And the enemy is gunning for you. What can you do? Let's look within this story from 1 Kings 20 to find out. A soldier tells a king how he had been given explicit orders to guard a particular prisoner. The soldier had been warned that "if by any means he is missing, your life shall be for his life, or else you shall pay a talent of silver" (verse 39).

The soldier in this passage had one job. He was to guard what looked to be a prisoner. The King James Version says it this way: "Keep this man." The Hebrew word for *keep* is *shamar*, which means "to hedge about (as with thorns), i.e., guard; generally, to protect, attend to, etc."[2] The original word captured the image of a sheepfold, a corral made out of thornbushes that shepherds used to protect their flocks from predators.[3] The soldier was told not to get distracted, and to protect the prisoner as he would a flock of his own sheep.

When the battle was over and the king and the soldier crossed paths, the story took a dark turn. The soldier told the king that he had lost the prisoner. I find the resulting exchange between the king and the soldier fascinating.

"How could this happen?" I imagine the king demanded. "What was so important that it distracted you from keeping the one man that was most important? Explain yourself!"

I'm sure the king expected the soldier to have a legitimate excuse on hand. Maybe, the king imagined, the soldier had been held at sword point by the enemy and had no choice but to cut the prisoner loose.

The soldier's response? "Your servant was busy here and there" (verse 40). He wasn't lazy. He wasn't a terrible soldier. He was, however, attacked by weapons of mass distraction. And his consequence was severe. Since he had lost the prisoner, he would lose his own life.

Personal holiness is the battle of the twenty-first-century believer in every life stage. As we seek holiness, we must take account of both our inner selves and our outer selves. Our outer self consists of the flesh and all the fleshly desires, and our inner self is the internal place in our hearts where the Holy Spirit is enthroned. We have to guard both our outer and inner selves with diligence. Our battlefield is the world we live in, along with the skirmishes we experience day by day in our hearts and minds. Distraction is a powerful weapon that the enemy uses to remove our focus from what really matters—that we become more and more like Jesus every day.

Just as the battlefield is noisy, so is our world. I'm not just talking about the world at large, but the world we've constructed around our individual lives—including our social networks, our responsibilities, our hobbies, our passions, our pastimes, our mental health and our physical priorities. The wonders of technology have turned us into screen zombies. We enroll our children in every activity under the sun. We overload our calendar and overwhelm our margin. The things we do are not all bad. Going to the gym a few times a week or watching your child kick the soccer ball around are good things! And social media can provide a wonderful means of connection with people we are far away from. But I find that as we saddle our days with nonstop activities, without intentionally guarding our inner selves, we empty our souls of what's most important.

Busy here, busy there; this has to be done, that has to be done. As days turn into weeks, your focus gets lost in the cares of the day. It starts slowly. Soon you forget your given task in this battle.

Your charge, in the midst of your warfare with the enemy, is to guard your relationship with Jesus. As believers, our number one assignment is to love the Lord our God with all our mind, heart, soul and strength. Next, we love our neighbor (everyone else), but this sacrificial act depends on us and our personal relationship with Jesus Christ.

King Solomon expressed the importance of tending to our relationship with God in Song of Solomon 1:6: "They made me the keeper of the vineyards, but my own vineyard I have not kept." He was evaluating all the mistakes he had made in his own life, looking at his own family that had been destroyed. Sometimes, God gives us responsibility for others and we put them first, thinking that we will be judged and evaluated by how well we do with looking after our "others." But the Lord needs to remain our focus first and foremost. Everything else flows from this relationship. If your relationship with God goes untended, as Solomon expresses, the other vineyards you are responsible for will spoil.

Do not get distracted. If you do, you will lose this relationship with God, and thus, you will lose yourself. It starts off small and slow, and then gradually, if you are not careful, the drift will pick up steam. Before you know it, you are thinking less and less about your relationship with God and are focusing on worldly pursuits and pleasures. By looking within, you are to guard who you are and your relationship with your Lord and Savior, above all.

Again, the soldier in the story wasn't a bad man. He was a busy man. He may even have been trying to accomplish things for his family and provide them with a certain lifestyle. Sound familiar? Most people don't mean to drift from God. We don't let our standards down and compromise on purpose. But when you remove the hedge of God's Word, His house and His people, and you get busy, there comes a day when you forget about your first love and, in the process, lose yourself.

The *W.A.T.C.H.* Principle

We live in days like none before. The signs of Jesus' return are everywhere you look. We are living in the age the prophets of old spoke about. It is both exciting and terrifying. But none of that will matter if Jesus looks at you on the day of judgment and says, "I knew you not."

Mark 13:32–37 offers such prophetic and powerful advice for the modern Church and for our lives today:

But of that day and hour no one knows, not even the angels in heaven, nor the Son, but only the Father. Take heed, watch and pray; for you do not know when the time is. It is like a man going to a far country, who left his house and gave authority to his servants, and to each his work, and commanded the doorkeeper to watch. Watch therefore, for you do not know when the master of the house is coming—in the evening, at midnight, at the crowing of the rooster, or in the morning—lest, coming suddenly, he finds you sleeping. And what I say to you, I say to all: Watch!

Take note of that last word, *watch*. In one of the letters Paul wrote to Timothy, he revealed what happens when we fail to watch: "Be diligent to come to me quickly; for Demas has forsaken me, having loved this present world, and has departed for Thessalonica" (2 Timothy 4:9–10). Though Demas is only mentioned three times in the Bible, he started strong in the ministry as an apprentice to the greatest preacher who ever lived, Paul. Demas traveled with Paul, shared the Good News and planted churches with him. And for a reason we don't know, Demas forsook Paul. Some translations use the word *deserted*. Though Demas started with good intentions and made valuable contributions, he misplaced his affections. He walked away from the faith because he loved the world more than he loved his Savior. If it could happen to Demas, it could happen to anyone.

I want to give you five aspects of your life that you need to W.A.T.C.H. in order to endure:

W—your Words
A—your Attitude
T—your Temptations
C—your Character
H—your Household

Watch Your Words—W

Words are very powerful. They can create or destroy, build up or tear down. "Death and life are in the power of the tongue, and those who love it will eat its fruit" (Proverbs 18:21). Every word you speak is a seed that is going forth and creating the future. You manifest what you say.

We need to send our words out in the direction we want them to go. In other words, we need to start talking victory when we're staring at defeat. We need to start talking healing when we're feeling sick. We need to start speaking blessing when we're running on empty. We need to start speaking about marching when we feel like quitting.

Jesus told us this:

Have faith in God. For assuredly, I say to you, whoever says to this mountain, "Be removed and be cast into the sea," and does not doubt in his heart, but believes that those things he says will be done, he will have whatever he says. Therefore I say to you, whatever things you ask when you pray, believe that you receive them, and you will have them.

Mark 11:22–24

Jesus emphasized the importance of what we say. Watching our words will sometimes even mean that we don't use words at all. There are times in our lives when the wisest thing we can do is to say nothing. When Jesus stood before Pilate, He used silence as a tool. He knew words would do no good in that moment. Your power in a situation may come from your silence, not your speech.

Words of death, depression, dysfunction and despair come from many places, including the enemy, those around us and our own hearts. Satan will whisper in your ear and tell you things that are not of God. He will remind you of your addiction and tell you that you are never going to get free. Or he will tell you that nobody could love a mess like you, not even God. Or that if people only knew the real you, no one would want to stand by your side. Never speak words that allow the enemy to think he's winning. Begin, today, to recognize those words that are coming your way from him. Look out for when those words appear in what you watch and hear.

Also watch the words that others say around you. You don't have to repeat negative reports. Nor do you have to share someone's lousy attitude or fearful behavior. Don't make your ears a garbage can. Watch the words that come your way from other people.

God knows that our peace of mind is tied to words. His Word asks, "Who has believed our report? And to whom has the arm of the LORD been revealed?" (Isaiah 53:1). In the Bible, the "arm of the LORD" refers to God's power to deliver and His providential care over every event in our lives. Are you going to listen to the words of God, His report of salvation?

> Don't make your ears a garbage can. Watch the words that come your way from other people.

Today, when you hear the message of the enemy creeping in, I want you to declare this aloud: "You're not coming in here! I have another report that says I'm loved by God. Christ shed His blood for my deliverance, and God has a purpose and plan for my life—and it's good!"

God is coming for your words this week. What will He find? The power of life and death are held in *your* tongue.

Watch Your Attitude—A

Just because bad things happen doesn't mean you need to be upset all the time. Satan has an original plan A—to keep people from getting saved. If that plan doesn't work, Satan has a plan B—to make you feel miserable. Our attitude in difficult circumstances is more important than what happens to us. As Philippians 2:5 tells us, "Let this mind be in you which was also in Christ Jesus."

I remember one beautiful day when my family and I were riding horses. All of a sudden, Cherise's horse bucked and she fell off. Although she was injured, it could have been much worse. She could have been paralyzed. She could have had a head injury. I marveled at her attitude. She didn't throw a tantrum, nor did she complain. She accepted the accident for what it was and chose to have a good attitude the rest of the day and throughout her recovery.

Sometimes, the horse unexpectedly bucks and you fall off. You get dirty, your plans get ruined, maybe you even sprain your ankle. It's easy to get angry or look for someone or something to blame. Yet a bad attitude is like a flat tire. You can't get very far until you change it!

The state of your attitude is a choice. Choose wisely. Refuse to be a negative, angry, mean person who can always find something to complain about. Fill yourself up with faith, hope and love. Live as if you have a sense of eternal purpose—because you do!

Watch Your Temptations—T

A teenager approached his grandfather one day and said, "I'm really battling temptation, Grandpa. How old will I be before I won't be tempted?"

His grandfather replied, "I don't know. I'm only eighty!"

Temptation is a constant. No one is exempt from it. We're tempted to quit. We're tempted to return to things we overcame in the past. We're tempted to watch something that will spoil our spirits. We're tempted to overindulge, gossip, lie—the list is endless. As long as you're alive, even after you fast and pray, temptation will still be knocking on your door, and it's a persistent knock. Watch your temptations. They can cost you everything.

Sometimes we go where we've been warned not to go. We lower our standards and convictions and think, *Oh, I can stop when I want to stop. When it gets too dangerous, I can back off.* God will let you go where you want to go because you have free will. But remember this: Rather than having what you want, there will come a time when those temptations will have you. Look within and listen to that still, small voice of the Holy Spirit warning you to back off, or to go back home, or, as the Bible says, to run! Sin may thrill at first, but eventually it will kill.

Right now, you are being studied. You are being watched. The enemy is plotting and planning. You cannot afford to relax or let your guard down. You are wanted by hell, so you must be careful what and whom you allow into your life. Who has your ear? What parts of your heart remain unguarded? What are you watching or listening to? What habits or behaviors are limiting your destiny?

I saw a documentary not too long ago about professional snake handlers who milk snakes for their venom. In order to qualify for this job, you must hold a degree in biology, chemistry, biochemistry or herpetology (the study of reptiles). If you're wondering why on earth anyone would even think about milking a snake, it's because venom plays a critical role in creating antivenom. Venom is also used in some medicines for strokes and cancer. In this documentary, some trainees were watching a professional snake handler milk a snake. The handler explained that most snakebites happen not when you pick the snake up, but when you put it down. This warning reminded me of how careful we must be with what we pick up!

It's easy to pick up a bad habit, isn't it? The Bible tells us about "the little foxes that spoil the vines" (Song of Solomon 2:15). A little bit of pornography, maybe once a month at first . . . Or a little drinking, just some wine on Friday evenings to unwind after a hard week . . . Or maybe losing interest in attending church or a small group, and just skipping a service here or there . . . Or maybe we start going a few places that aren't going to help us become the best version of ourselves . . .

It's not the bear, the lion or the wolf that destroys the vine; it's the little fox that nibbles it away, one chew and swallow at a time. And the more you do these things, the more deeply entrenched you become. When it's time to put them down, it's not so easy.

Remember, you are an overcomer. You don't have to surrender to lusts of the flesh. (In chapter 12, we'll talk more about that.) Jesus was tempted, but He endured and withstood the enemy. He has overcome the devil and every trap of the enemy. And because He has overcome, you can be free of every bad habit or addiction.

Watch Your Character—C

You can lead without character, but you won't be a leader worth following. Your character will always outweigh your position. If you say you're going to do something for someone, do it. If you promise someone you'll be there at 5:00 p.m., show up on time. If you volunteer to help a friend move, don't bail out at the last minute just because it may not have been the best idea to begin with. Character matters.

When Abraham and Sarah were visiting a place called Gerar, the king of that region, Abimelech, took one look at Sarah and fell into lust (see Genesis 20). Even though a harem of beautiful women surrounded him every day, he couldn't take his eyes off Sarah. By the way, she was 99 years old at the time. I think we all want to take whatever she was having!

Abraham didn't want to get in trouble with the king, so he lied and said Sarah was his sister. Sarah went along with the fib. The king was pleased and arranged for Sarah to visit him in his palace. That night, before King Abimelech even touched Sarah, God came to the king in a dream. God was furious and told him, "Indeed you are a dead man because of the woman whom you have taken, for she is a man's wife" (Genesis 20:3).

After King Abimelech picked up his mouth off the floor, he and the Lord had this conversation:

But Abimelech had not come near her; and he said, "Lord, will You slay a righteous nation also? Did he not say to me, 'She is my sister'? And she, even she herself said, 'He is my brother.' In the integrity of my heart and innocence of my hands I have done this."

And God said to him in a dream, "Yes, I know that you did this in the integrity of your heart. For I also withheld you from sinning against Me; therefore I did not let you touch her. Now therefore, restore the man's wife; for he is a prophet, and he will pray for you and you shall live. But if you do not restore her, know that you shall surely die, you and all who are yours."

Genesis 20:4–7

God is more interested in your character than your comfort. Examine your character. According to Proverbs 10:9, "He who walks with integrity walks securely, but he who perverts his ways will become known." It's always the right time to do what is right.

Watch Your Household—H

Besides God, there is nothing more precious to me than my family. And now my sons-in-law and grandkids. My family is worth more to me than silver or gold. They're worth more than any acclaim the world could ever offer and any title or position I could ever earn.

I understand that everyone has a different family dynamic. You might not be married, or you might be divorced and be sharing custody of your children. Maybe you're child-free by choice. But whatever our dynamic, we all have people who fall into the circle we call our household. Whether you have kids or not, choose to invest in the next generation.

Don't become so preoccupied with schedules and routines, and so overwhelmed with responsibilities—I know there are many!—that your priority to love and serve your family gets left behind.

Today, being busy seems to equal success. Many of us complain about being time poor and lacking the energy and hours it takes to invest in our relationships with our spouse and children. Make time for your family. Play with them. Take them out for no particular reason. Listen to them more than you talk. Instead of just taking them to church on Sundays, show them the love of Christ during the week.

The Bible tells us that Abraham's nephew Lot was once kidnapped. Lot's father, Abraham's brother, had died, so Abraham took in Lot as if he were his own son. When Lot was captured by five enemy armies, Abraham knew that if he tried to coordinate a rescue attempt, he would be far outnumbered. But he did it anyway. Abraham was willing to pay any price to get his nephew back—and with God's grace, his plan worked.

> **When you pray and stand on God's Word, you are wielding two of God's greatest weapons not only for yourself, but also for your household.**

Pray for your children, your nephews and nieces, your friends' children and those children you teach or watch. Determine that these children will be fruitful in the Kingdom of God and that hell will not have them, in Jesus' name. When you pray and stand on God's Word, you are wielding two of God's greatest weapons not only for yourself, but also for your household.

Beware of Satan's Greatest Attack: Offense

Along with standing W.A.T.C.H., there is something we also must vigilantly guard against: offense. In these end times, I see Satan's attack on believers and nonbelievers alike through the spirit of offense.

Offense is running rampant through the Church. Through offense, the enemy is constantly trying to derail the victorious life of the believer. Jesus warned us of this very thing:

And then many will be offended, will betray one another, and will hate one another. Then many false prophets will rise up and deceive many. And because lawlessness will abound, the love of many will grow cold. But he who endures to the end shall be saved.

Matthew 24:10–13

I'm sure you know at least one person who has stopped attending church or listening to anything related to Jesus because he or she was offended by something a Christian said or did. Maybe the person felt insulted because the pastor of a church he or she was visiting talked about tithing. Maybe it was hearing news of yet another church leader involved in a scandal. Maybe this person didn't like a teaching in the Bible because it seemed antiquated.

The New Testament alludes seventeen times to someone being offended, while the word *offense* is mentioned sixteen times. One of the main words translated into English as *offense* in the New Testament is the Greek word *skandalon*. It is defined as "properly, the trigger of a trap (the mechanism closing a trap down on the unsuspecting victim); (figuratively) an *offense*, putting *a negative cause-and-effect relationship* into motion."[4] Satan is always setting traps for you to fall into. He wants to get you offended so he can rob you of the miracles Jesus wants to do for you.

Two verses in the gospel of Matthew speak powerfully to the dangerous effects of offense in the life of a believer. First, in explaining the parable of the sower, Jesus says in Matthew 13:20–21,

But he who received the seed on stony places, this is he who hears the word and immediately receives it with joy; yet he has no root in himself, but endures only for a while. For when tribulation or persecution arises because of the word, immediately he stumbles.

In the King James Version, the wording "he stumbles" is translated this way: "he is offended." Next, we have Matthew 13:53–58:

> Now it came to pass, when Jesus had finished these parables, that He departed from there. When He had come to His own country, He taught them in their synagogue, so that they were astonished and said, "Where did this Man get this wisdom and these mighty works? Is this not the carpenter's son? Is not His mother called Mary? . . . Where then did this Man get all these things?" So they were offended at Him.
>
> But Jesus said to them, "A prophet is not without honor except in his own country and in his own house." Now He did not do many mighty works there because of their unbelief.

In these two passages in particular, the Word of God shows that when you move into the place of offense, the miracles stop. The Holy Spirit may be moving in a church, but if people there are harboring offense in their hearts, the Spirit will shut down a supernatural move of God. Leave the justice and vengeance and righteousness to God. Don't miss your miracle because of offense.

When David volunteered to fight Goliath, his brothers got jealous and started yelling insults at him and taunting him. His oldest brother, Eliab, angrily demanded, "Why did you come down here? And with whom have you left those few sheep in the wilderness? I know your pride and the insolence of your heart, for you have come down to see the battle" (1 Samuel 17:28). These brothers preferred for David to stay in his lane and tend sheep rather than battle against a giant. David had to step over the offense of his brothers belittling him. He didn't acknowledge it. If he had, it could have robbed him of the miracle of slaying Goliath.

You'll never kill the giant in your life until you first let go of offense. Then God will begin to fight your battles for you.

As he awaited execution in prison, John the Baptist sent word via his disciples to Jesus to ask if He was indeed the Messiah (see Matthew 11:2–3). Here was John's reasoning: If Christ was the miracle-working Messiah, He would have the power to get John out of prison. If Christ was not the one, then John's ministry was incomplete, and he would somehow be released to continue preaching to his wilderness congregation at the Jordan River, until the correct Messiah appeared.

Jesus told John's disciples to go back to John and tell him that the blind were seeing, the deaf were hearing, the lepers were being cleansed, the dead were being raised, and the poor were receiving the Gospel (see verses 4–5). Jesus then delivered a powerful statement for John's disciples to relay to him: "And blessed is he who is not offended because of Me" (verse 6).

John did not die offended at Christ. We must not die with offenses in our hearts. When the answers we get do not meet our expectations, we must trust that God knows about our situation and is still working all things out for our good.

Like John, the apostle Paul also learned to move beyond offense. A group of zealous Jewish men hated Paul because they detested his conversion to Christ. This group brought false charges against him, accusing him before the authorities of creating dissension, profaning the Temple and being a mover of sedition among all the Jewish people in the world (see Acts 24:5–6). These charges required Paul to stand before the governor and defend himself. He had been lied about and verbally abused, and these vicious men had assaulted his character. Yet Paul bore no ill will. In fact, he said in his statement of defense, "I myself always strive to have a conscience without offense toward God and men" (Acts 24:16).

How do you know you're holding onto an offense? If you make a habit of still talking and thinking about what happened to you or who hurt you, and if you long for revenge, you are still carrying an offense. How can you let go of this offense? Nobody can do it for you. Just as nobody can do your sit-ups and push-ups for you. The word *exercise* means to train, and by implication alludes to striving for something. Staying offense-free is something you must train your mind and spirit to do, always striving to keep your conscience clear from the brain fog produced by offenses. If you don't have a healthy spirit, you have to look within. Ask God to create in you a clean heart and a right spirit (see Psalm 51:10). He will do it. He always does.

The Remedy: Forgive

Because offenses will be evident in the last days, we need to know the biblical solution for offense—forgiveness. Forgiveness brings freedom. If you have been offended and want to be free from Satan's greatest attack, you must take the high road and forgive, again and again—season after season.

Forgiveness is so important that there is a line in the Lord's Prayer that says, "Forgive us our debts, as we forgive our debtors" (Matthew 6:12 KJV). The Greek word translated as debt here, *opheiléma*, is not just something owed; it also refers to some type of a moral fault.[5]

To forgive another person who has offended you is not optional; it's a command. Because the Lord has forgiven us, removing our sins and granting us the free gift of eternal life, He requires us to forgive others. We forgive just as we have been forgiven (see Colossians 3:13). Christ warned that if we do not forgive our brothers or sisters their trespasses against us, then our heavenly Father will not forgive us our trespasses (see Matthew 6:15). Even our financial gifts will not be blessed if we are giving with a heart of unforgiveness, as it says in Matthew 5:23–24: "Therefore, if you bring your gift to the altar, and there remember that your brother has something against you, leave your gift there before the altar, and go your way. First be reconciled to your brother, and then come and offer your gift."

Jesus said, "But he that shall endure unto the end, the same shall be saved" (Matthew 24:13 KJV). The Greek word *endure* used in this passage is *hupomeno*, which means "to stay under (behind), i.e. remain; figuratively, to undergo, i.e. bear (trials), have fortitude, persevere:—abide, endure, (take) patient(-ly), suffer, tarry behind."[6] When you have been offended or betrayed, you must be able to bear up under the emotional and spiritual impact. If you can forgive an offense and not retaliate or become angry and resentful, you will develop an attitude of forgiveness. I don't expect anyone not to be hurt or feel disappointed or betrayed when he or she has been wronged. Forgiveness isn't easy and requires internal work! But forgiveness is a remedy to offense, and it will always provide healing and freedom.

If you allow an offense to fester, it will become a powerful weapon in the hand of your adversary, Satan. An offended spirit gives the enemy a foothold—something to hold onto in your daily life. When you release others who have hurt you and move on, you seize the strength of the weapon from the hand of the adversary.

Forgiveness can be difficult. We forgive others to bring renewal and refreshment by breaking the hold that the offense and the offender had over us. As long as we refuse to forgive our offender, that person still has a knife in our heart. When we choose to forgive others and tarry (or take the time) to commune with God, a transaction takes place within our soul. Jesus will remove the anger, pain, hatred, hurt, embarrassment and bitterness from us and replace those things with a greater portion of the rewards that we can receive through His Spirit—rewards like healing, gladness, joy and an inheritance in God.

Schedule Spiritual Check-Ins

We will all fight internal battles in this life. Before we ask God for answers to the problems that plague us on this earth, we have a duty to self-reflect. We must look inward first. Sometimes the time we spend judging others or begging God for signs or explanations is best spent on an inner assessment. Are we living with the same integrity in private that we are in public? Are we guarding our heart from that which can destroy us? What is coming out of our mouth—doom and gloom, or hope and revival?

When Jesus told the parable of the sower and the seeds, the seeds had one of four outcomes. Some seeds fell by the wayside, some fell on stony ground, some took root in good ground at first, but then were choked out by thorns. Finally, some seeds fell on good ground. Three out of four groups of seeds didn't make it. Only one group stayed rooted in good ground and remained productive, not just for a season, but for longevity.

As you run to the finish line, take time to examine yourself. An airplane flying just one degree off its assigned flight plan can end up hundreds of miles from its destination. And if it's out of fuel, well, it's only going one place—down.

Schedule time for spiritual check-ins. Yes, watch for the return of the Lord so that you are ready. But watch what you can control, change and develop now. W.A.T.C.H. yourself! And remember to take Step #1 that will help you overcome:

LOOK WITHIN

> For the Lord does not see as man sees;
> for man looks at the outward appearance,
> but the Lord looks at the heart.
>
> **1 SAMUEL 16:7**

4

Step #2: Look to Him

Tino Wallenda is the sixth generation of wire walkers in the Wallenda family—high-wire circus performers who do not use safety nets. Their legacy began in the late 1700s, when Tino's family started out as a traveling circus troupe in Europe. Eventually, they focused their expertise on high-wire acts and became known as The Flying Wallendas. This famous family is named in the *Guinness Book of World Records* for their eight-person pyramid up on the wire.

Tino has walked the wire between high-rise buildings, the tallest being the Denver D&F Tower, a reach of 189 feet into the air. He walked to the tower from a crane that was set up 3,300 feet away. He has also walked the wire over rivers, over waterfalls, over tigers and once over a swimming pool filled with more than fifty man-eating sharks.

Tino's grandfather, Karl Wallenda, who crossed Tallulah Falls Gorge and performed two headstands in the middle of that walk, taught Tino how to maintain balance on the wire. Tino says of his grandfather,

Staying focused on Jesus is the key, no matter who you are. It's just like what my grandfather Karl taught me about walking the wire. The most important thing he ever taught me was to put my focus on an unmoving point at the far end of the wire and never let my attention waver. Over and over again, he drilled into my thick skull the importance of maintaining my balance by focusing on this fixed point. That lesson has saved me from disaster on the tightrope so many times in my career—but it has also helped me in my day-to-day life.[1]

The minute life gets overwhelming, we tend to stop looking at Jesus and we focus more on the problem. We can't stop thinking about the addiction that's ravaging our brain space and destroying our marriage. Or the anxiety that forces us to stay in bed all day. Yet the moment you gave your life to Jesus, He began to direct your path (see Proverbs 3:5–6). And while His plan for you would include storms, it also provides a rescue. Life requires faith to endure the storms. Once I heard someone say that we're either in a storm, on our way into a storm or getting out of a storm. I have a feeling that if you are reading this book, you are familiar with stormy weather in a metaphorical sense. I have often reached the verge of disaster because my eyes were on the storm, not on the fixed point, Jesus.

Wherever you are right now, I have a word for you. The message God wants every believer to embrace is what Jesus told the disciples in Matthew 24:6: "See that you are not troubled." That might be hard to do when you're nursing a broken heart, when the rent is due and the bank account is insufficient, when you're in recovery for the third time. But the words of Jesus hold the same power today as when He spoke them to His disciples. The scene may be different, but the truth has not changed. Not one bit. Through all the fear, anxiety and confusion in your heart right now, abide in His words: "See that you are not troubled."

How do you do that? Keep your eyes on Jesus. The best advice I can offer you is Step #2, *look to Him.*

Lessons in Survival

Looking to Jesus is the gold standard for surviving the storms of life. It's what Peter discovered when he stepped out of the boat and began to walk on the water toward Jesus. I want to use this story as an anchor for this second step to overcoming in the end times, *look to Him*.

The gospels record the story of the day Jesus made His disciples get in a boat and go to the other side of the Sea of Galilee. When I first went to Israel and stood before the famous Sea of Galilee, I thought the bus had arrived at the wrong location! It was not a sea as I had imagined it, like the Atlantic or Pacific Oceans, with an endless view of water and no land in sight. The Sea of Galilee seemed small to me, more like a large lake. It is shaped like a harp and is about thirteen miles long and eight miles wide. But perhaps it is called a sea because of the types of storms that can suddenly strike the water, creating waves as high as three to four feet. The tempests arrive when the cooler air masses from the surrounding mountains collide with the warm air above the lake. Fierce winds can also blow in from the eastern Golan Heights.

I witnessed this type of turbulent behavior firsthand. I had just finished preaching a message on the Sea of Galilee (literally) when the captain said, "Everyone, we have to go right now!" Only minutes later, one of the most intense storms I have ever seen came out of nowhere. The abrupt storm helped me understand how the disciples felt that day.

As the disciples sailed off, Jesus stayed behind, going up the mountain to pray in solitude. When evening came, a storm erupted on the water. The disciples battled the winds and the waves all night. When it was the fourth and last watch, around 3:00 a.m. in the morning, the petrified men, wet to the skin, saw what looked like a ghost walking on the water. It was Jesus. I imagine that the disciples, wiping stinging water from their eyes, were trying hard not to hyperventilate at this peculiar sight. Then Jesus called out to them, "Be of good cheer! It is I; do not be afraid" (Matthew 14:27).

At the sight of Jesus, Peter grew bold. He asked Jesus to command him to come and walk on the violent seas. Jesus told Peter to come, and the disciple edged out of the teetering vessel. I imagine shock swept over the drenched man as the churning waves roiled over his feet, the rain coming in sideways. A few steps ahead, the fierce breath of the wind almost robbed him of his balance. Fear struck his heart, and Peter began to sink.

Immediately, Jesus caught him and said, "O you of little faith, why did you doubt?" (verse 31). As the two climbed aboard the vessel that rocked from one side to the other atop the agitated sea, suddenly there was peace. The waves lulled to rest. The wind stopped its piercing howl. And the rain ceased.

Though it may have felt like it to the disciples, Jesus hadn't left them alone in the storm. He was with them on the water just as much as He was with them while He was praying on the side of the mountain. Jesus wasn't blind or distracted. He had seen what had happened, from the moment the disciples began to row past the shallow shores to the moment the storm clouds fractured the skies. And He showed up in physical form right on time.

Don't take your eyes off Jesus; look to Him. He's got you!

I bring you good news—Jesus hasn't gone anywhere. Just as He was with Peter when Peter walked on water, He is right here to save you. Maybe you're weighed down by guilt over years wasted, or you're encumbered with fear because the news on your newsfeed spits out nothing but negativity, violence and despair. Take a breath. Right now. Your hope is not gone. Your future is secure. The set of circumstances you find yourself in is but a season, not a sentence.

Don't take your eyes off Jesus; look to Him. He's got you!

Rowing by Divine Instruction

Here's something that strikes me when I read this story of walking on water: Jesus *made* the disciples go to the other side. The King James Version puts it like this: "Jesus constrained his disciples to get into a ship, and to go before him unto the other side" (Matthew 14:22). *Constrained* is a strong word. Jesus didn't give these guys a choice. He made them go. They weren't in the middle of a storm because they had messed up or failed somehow. They were there because of divine instruction.

Jesus put them in the storm. He knew that they would receive revelations in the storm that they would never learn from the safety of the shore.

Know that if you are reading this book today and the winds are howling and the waves are raging in your life, God didn't create the storm to hurt you. He has allowed you to be exactly where you are in order to show you things that you can only learn in a storm. Even when you make poor decisions and create storms yourself that you could have avoided, God is still with you. He is telling you today, *I am the God who has a superseding rule over your life, called "divine instruction," and even out of this struggle, you will overcome.*

The most critical thing you can do in a storm is keep rowing. When his newborn son died in 2011, P. J. Fleck, the current football coach (as of this writing) for the University of Minnesota's Golden Gophers, developed a mantra for approaching life during that terrible storm. He called it "Row the Boat." Describing this new life perspective, Fleck says,

> Your back is to the future, which is something you cannot control. . . . You don't know if there's rocks, water falls, stormy seas, you don't know what's ahead of you. You're rowing in the present, which is the only thing you can actually control, and the only thing you can actually have an impact on. You either choose to take your oars and

put them back in the boat and stop, or you put them back in the water and continue to go.[2]

Coach Fleck refers to the oars as the energy, a symbol of strength. I like to think that the oars that are needed to persevere and overcome in a storm are worship and faith.

Satan wants you to drop your oars and give up. He wants you to just throw up your hands in despair and ask, *What's the use?* He will distract you from listening to worshipful music or powerful messages about faith because he knows the power found in those two things—power that can move a mountain and still a storm.

As you look to Jesus in any storm, focus on the promises of God. His promises reinforce your faith. Think of Job and all he went through when he lost his nest of comfort and stability. His natural reaction may have been to give up, but he used the two oars of worship and faith to hang in there and trust in God.

When God watches you worship, He sees you activating your faith. He takes notice of how you push through discouragement and give Him glory. And that's when He shows up. When the family situation is tough, the financial challenges are overwhelming, and the sickness just seems too much to bear, take a breath and lift your hands. Say, *God, here I am. I'm moving forward. I'm still rowing with my oars of worship and faith. And I will not quit until You show up.*

You don't have to impress God with big words. Exhale your faith through your words, in whatever simple language you need to use. This is how you row, one stroke at a time.

Sometimes the wind is at your back, and it feels as if everything's going for you. You're doing all the right things, and you may think the outcome will be God's favor and blessings lavished on you. But other times, the wind is blowing directly in your face, and it feels as if everything's going against you. Don't ever let the direction of the wind determine whether you believe God is with you or not. He is always with you, and just because things are coming against you does not mean you're doing anything wrong. Row the boat. Keep on rowing.

The disciples didn't stop rowing—and Jesus saw that. This is key. The disciples weren't doing nothing. They were fighting. Jesus saw them as they were straining and toiling, muscles aching, and He went to them (see Mark 6:48). I want you to know today that your inability to see Jesus doesn't mean that He can't see you. He saw the disciples rowing in the midst of a mighty storm, just as He sees you in the middle of your crisis. He is the God of provision on the shore and the God of miracles in the midst of your storms. Just as the disciples rowed with all their might, you can use the oars of worship and faith to row, knowing they will get you to where God needs you to go.

> Don't ever let the direction of the wind determine whether you believe God is with you or not.

Proverbs 15:3 says the eyes of the Lord are everywhere, beholding the evil and the good. God sees the times you slip and fall into sin, but He also sees the good in your life. He sees the righteousness of Jesus in you. He sees your faith and praise. He sees your willingness not to give up. He sees you believing and holding on. Your God sees the good, and that should bring great comfort. Believe in the promise that He won't ever leave or forsake you. He will never abandon you in the storm.

Keep worshiping. Keep believing. Don't give up.

I don't know what deliverance from a storm will look like for you. You might walk on water. You might stay in the boat. You might get to the other side with the sea still raging. Don't carve your own way out. Trust God to do it His way.

Sometimes, you don't really find out who Jesus is until you get into a storm. You don't really find out how faithful, loving and merciful He is until you are in desperate need of a Savior. Maybe you are in a storm right now and there seems to be no sign of Jesus yet. Just keep looking for Him. He is going to come walking on top of the challenge that is about to take you under, and He will calm your storm in such a way that the only reasonable response is to worship Him and declare, *You really are the Son of God!*

The most powerful lesson from the entire story of the disciples facing the storm is not found in the miracle of Peter being able to walk on water. It is found in the profound revelation of who Jesus really is. The miracle is not always the revelation.

The feeding of thousands wasn't the first miracle the disciples ever saw. They had seen water turn into wine, sight be restored to the blind. They had watched crooked limbs straighten and had witnessed demons coming out of people. But their doubts still simmered. They didn't understand who Jesus was. It took a terrifying storm to see not only His power, but also His authority. They finally had a fuller picture of the One they had committed to follow. As He stretched out His hand, waves crashing at His robe, and ceased the wind from blowing, everyone in the boat recognized that Jesus was the Son of God. Who He is, is always greater than what He does.

Pick Up the Bread Crumbs

When your arms are achy, numbed or fatigued from rowing, think back and remember all the times God has come to your rescue. Prior to Jesus telling the disciples to get into the boat, another miracle had occurred. We read in Mark 6:30–44 that Jesus was speaking to a crowd of close to ten thousand people. Mark records five thousand men in number, but that number would at least be doubled if the women and children were counted. It was getting close to dinnertime, and the crowd started getting hungry. Jesus miraculously used a little boy's lunch of five fish and two loaves of bread to feed everyone—plus twelve baskets of leftovers remained! Then Jesus dismissed everyone and made the disciples take their divinely appointed boat trip.

After Peter had walked on water and had almost slipped under and drowned, we read that when he and Jesus got back into the boat, the disciples "were greatly amazed in themselves beyond measure, and marveled. For they had not understood about the loaves, because their heart was hardened" (Mark 6:51–52). In other words, they didn't understand the miracle they had witnessed before the storm as an example of how they could trust that Jesus would provide. Think about it. The miracle of Jesus feeding thousands of people had happened only a few hours earlier. We are so quick to forget the positive.

As the disciples were battered by winds and beaten by waves, I'm sure their fingers still smelled like fish and their bellies still stuffed from carbs. If Jesus could feed thousands with a lunch made for one kid, could He not save them from these elements of the weather? And if Jesus could give Peter the power to walk on the stormy sea, was He not able to sustain this disciple to walk a few steps farther so he could stand alongside Jesus while the weather raged? That's why, when Peter began to slip into the sea, Jesus said, "O you of little faith, why did you doubt?" (Matthew 14:31).

Jesus wanted Peter to remember the fish and the loaves of bread, reminders that He could provide. And that's what I mean when I say "pick up the bread crumbs." Never forget what God has done for you. Let those memories fuel you when you're knocked off your feet by an unforgiving wave.

Difficult seasons come. The economy collapses, a loved one gets sick, you lose your job, the medicine doesn't temper your anxiety, a string of bad decisions evolves into a mental breakdown. Sometimes the storm is our fault, and sometimes it's not. But when you're in a place where you know you need a miracle, pick up the bread crumbs from the last miracle. Remember how God kept you from going bankrupt or gave you the strength to carry on when you had lost something or someone you loved. Remember the faithfulness He showed you when you didn't deserve it at all.

If you take the time to breathe and reflect, you can remember that God will not let you go. If you're facing trouble, close your eyes and fix your sight on Jesus' nail-pierced palms, and remember that He willingly gave His life for yours.

A Second Storm

In addition to the story of Peter walking on water, there is another well-known storm the gospel of Luke records. The same cast of characters was present, but with a whole new lesson to learn. Luke 8 records the time Jesus got into a boat on the same sea and invited the disciples to take a ride "over to the other side of the lake" (Luke 8:22). In the Greek, this phrase "other side" is a derivative of the word *peiro*, which means to "pierce," "beyond, on the other side" or "cross."[3] I see a spiritual nugget hidden in Jesus' statement: To get to where we need to be will require a piercing through of circumstances that hinder us.

As the disciples began to row across the lake, Jesus fell asleep. And as the weather turned and the sky blackened and emptied its fury, He continued to snooze. Luke 8:23 tells us that by that point, the disciples were in jeopardy. The boat was taking on water. This was turning into a life-or-death situation. Yet Jesus was sleeping. How could this be? Why didn't He wake up and join in the panic? I believe it's because He knew His word had already been spoken over the situation. Prior to embarking onto the boat, He had not said, "*I* am going to the other side." Instead, He had included His disciples: "Let *us* cross over to the other side." The *us* made the difference. The plan was to make it to the destination together.

The disciples came to Christ in fear, waking Him up and saying, "Master, Master, we are perishing!" (verse 24). Notice they said *we* are perishing, which appeared to exclude Jesus in this perishing process. They never said *you*: "You are about to perish. . . . You are about to die! Jesus, You are going under!" Perhaps they had faith for *Him* and no faith for *themselves*.

When the disciples awoke Jesus, He immediately "rebuked the wind and the raging of the water" (verse 24). The word *rebuked* carries the idea of censuring something, such as when Jesus rebuked demons, then forbade them to speak (see Luke 4:41). Rebuking the storm was Christ taking authority over the root cause of a conflict. He rebuked the wind and also the raging of the water. The word *raging* here indicates the violent dashing of the water against the vessel. Wooden vessels would be broken apart if this type of raging storm persisted. And afterward, Christ rebuked His disciples, asking them, "Where is your faith?" (Luke 8:25).

During the end times, many types of storms will be brewing in the nations, the Church and the world. Some storms will come and go swiftly, doing little or no harm. Others, however, will be well planned, with set targets. It will require faith to pass the tests and endure the storms.

No gust of wind, towering wave or blinding rain would have been strong enough, however, to keep the disciples from going where Jesus intended them to go. Know this today: You are going to the other side!

When we face our storms, we must look to Jesus. But how? What will that feel like? When David was overwhelmed, he would recall the miracles God had performed for Israel in Egypt and in the wilderness (see Psalm 103). When you have needs, always remember the stories you have heard of God's provision. When you are hit with a surprise sickness that appears devastating, recall the stories of healing that the Lord performed not only in the Bible, but throughout the generations of history. When the powers of darkness attack your children, focus on the promises God has given in His Word that if you train up children in the way they should go, when they are old, they will not depart from it (see Proverbs 22:6).

The stories of the storms of Galilee give us possible clues as to why we falter and feel overwhelmed, as if we are sinking. We are forgetting God's Word, and forgetting His miracles, and focusing on the circumstances. Stand on the Word in the middle of the storm and never forget what God has done in the past, since He can repeat the same miracles in the future.

What's on the Other Side

While some storms are sent to discourage you, other storms come because you have entered enemy territory and have attracted the attention of the forces of evil. Many times, these kinds of storms appear when you are close to a breakthrough or close to exposing lies. It's in times like these that you need to know who you are and Whose you are. Once you know who you are, the enemy has to recognize your identity, too. After forty days of fasting, Jesus was tempted by Satan over His identity. The devil said, "If You are the Son of God, command that these stones become bread" (Matthew 4:3). But Jesus knew who He was. He didn't have to turn stones into bread to prove His identity.

I believe that the storm Jesus and His disciples endured on the Sea of Galilee was not a natural storm; it was a demonic one. When He was approaching the area the demonic forces occupied, He knew He was entering enemy territory. The demons immediately recognized who Jesus was, and His mere presence caused such a violent reaction in the spirit world that a storm began to break out even before He arrived on shore. This was a holy area occupied by something unclean.

When you enter a territory the enemy occupies—which could mean anywhere from your school, to your office, to your neighborhood where you are witnessing to a neighbor—that's territory the enemy thinks belongs to him. Your mere presence, and the presence of the

Holy Spirit that you carry into that territory, can create a storm of fierce opposition. Rejoice because you are closer to your breakthrough than ever. The storm indicates that something big is about to happen.

The enemy's goal is to get your eyes off what's on the other side of the storm. Why? Because he knows your reward is on the other side. Not at the beginning of the trial, not in the middle of the struggle, when you get discouraged. Your reward is at the end.

Somewhere between sickness and healing, there's going to be a storm. Somewhere between poverty and provision, the storms will come. You may lose your job. Your car may break down. That's okay. It's all part of the victory process when you enter enemy territory. But the greater the opposition, the clearer your indication that God is about to set something loose.

The storm tells you that you're getting close.

Somewhere between your loved one being bound by sin and trusting in Jesus, you're going to see some confrontations. You're going to say some words you wish you could take back, see some tears shed. You're going to have fallouts and lockouts, cry crocodile tears and occasionally flip out. But I'm telling you, these are the signs that you are nearing the other side of the storm. In order to overcome the overwhelming, you must be willing to cross through chaos. The stronger the storm, the closer you are to the point of deliverance. Keep looking to Jesus.

LOOK TO HIM

Looking unto Jesus, the author and finisher of our faith, who for the joy that was set before Him endured the cross, despising the shame, and has sat down at the right hand of the throne of God.

HEBREWS 12:2

77

Step #3: Look Ahead

In my many years as a runner, I've learned an important secret about going for a successful run. I make up my mind before I start exactly how far I'm going to run. If I don't take that important step, my body will quickly decide that the run is over and not take any more steps. This secret to running is also a secret for living: Finishing the race requires knowing your end goal before you even take that first step.

Jesus told His disciples in Matthew 24:13, "But he who endures to the end shall be saved." Just as the secret to Tino Wallenda's balance on a high wire is to focus on a fixed point at the end of the wire, our job as believers is to maintain laser focus and fix our eyes on the prize, to stay the course laid before us.

He who endures to the end shall be saved. The one who lasts is the one who wins. It doesn't matter how long it takes or what you look like in the end. What matters is that you remain. To endure isn't always enjoyable or fun. Sometimes it's draining, unglamourous, even rote—but wait, we endure for a reason. We're not doing it just because. There is always a purpose, even in the pain.

Paul writes this about the reason we endure:

> Let us run with endurance the race that is set before us, looking unto Jesus, the author and finisher of our faith, who for the joy that was set before Him endured the cross, despising the shame, and has sat down at the right hand of the throne of God.
>
> For consider Him who endured such hostility . . . lest you become weary and discouraged.
>
> Hebrews 12:1–3

Jesus endured the cross because of the joy set before Him. He endured Calvary because He could look ahead and see the resurrection. Don't let what is going on around you sabotage what God is doing within you. Instead of feeling frustrated at where you are, focus on where you are going. Remember these words that Paul wrote:

> Therefore do not cast away your confidence, which has great reward. For you have need of endurance, so that after you have done the will of God, you may receive the promise:
>
> For yet a little while, and He who is coming will come and will not tarry.
>
> Hebrews 10:35–37

Determine that no matter what you must endure, you will not give up in this hard time.

Six Ways to Look Ahead

The chaos of life can block our view of the hope before us. How can we endure when we can't see past this afternoon? We all face moments when enduring seems impossible. I want to give you six different ways to build up your endurance so that if the kind of moment comes when carrying on just seems impossible, you are ready to embrace the resistance and push through it. Here are six ways to put into practice Step #3, *look ahead*:

1. Create the right atmosphere.
2. Connect to the right power supply.
3. Get the right information.
4. Get in the right location.
5. Get the right focus.
6. Get the right timing.

Let's look at each of these ways to look ahead and endure a little more closely.

1. Create the right atmosphere.

In life, you create the atmosphere. In a word, the right atmosphere is praise. Have you ever noticed that emotions create atmospheres? If somebody is sad, you walk into the room and you feel that sadness. If somebody is fearful, you can feel that. If somebody is angry or upset about something, without a word being said, that person projects a negative feeling from his or her spirit into the atmosphere of a room, just from the anger he or she possesses.

There's an amazing story in the Old Testament about King Saul. If Saul were alive today, he probably would be diagnosed as bipolar. He had fits and times when darkness and depression would come on him and he would go out of his mind. And the Bible tells us that when the evil spirits of depression troubled him and he went into the dark place of his life, he would do something strange. He'd call David and ask him to come over with his harp and fill the palace with soothing music. And the young boy would play his music as the king sat on the throne in depression, in darkness, in the sorrow of life and in hopelessness. All David did was fill the room with praise, and it would change the atmosphere of the place. The evil spirits would depart from Saul, and he would return again to a place of peace in his life.

You may not be able to change your circumstance, but you can control the atmosphere. Think of the type of people you are associating with, and think about the content you are consuming. Are they positive or negative? Faith-filled or fear-filled? What sort of atmosphere are you creating with the words coming out of your mouth or the thoughts filling your mind?

When you decide to change your atmosphere, you can shift the trajectory of your day from worry to worship, from panic to praise.

2. Connect to the right power supply.

The right energy source for a believer is the Holy Spirit. When you accepted Jesus Christ as your Lord and Savior, the Holy Spirit came to live inside you. In short, this is the indwelling of the Spirit. He will speak to your heart as you go through the highs and lows of this life. In John 14:26, Jesus calls the Holy Spirit the Helper and says, "He will teach you all things, and bring to your remembrance all things that I said to you." Though we cannot physically see Him, the Holy Spirit is our helper and our teacher. So this isn't about a God way up there whom you go see on Sundays or when you are in trouble. This is a constant companion. The Holy Spirit is with you always and everywhere you go. This was God's plan when He took Jesus back to heaven to sit at His right hand, praying for you. This Holy Spirit is called your teacher, counselor, helper, comforter, close friend and protector.

I had the opportunity to visit the Upper Room in Jerusalem. Two thousand plus years earlier, in what may have been that same room or a room that looked like it, a group of 120 people gathered. They were the first to receive the baptism of the Holy Spirit, but certainly not the last. This ordinary, run-of-the-mill group was equipped with power, strength and passion to fulfill the will of God for their lives. "But you shall receive power when the Holy Spirit has come upon you; and you shall be witnesses to Me in Jerusalem, and in all Judea and Samaria, and to the end of the earth" (Acts 1:8). As a result of what happened, the Bible says "that day about three thousand souls were added to them" (Acts 2:41).

What would this world look like if we were connected to that kind of power? The Bible says every nation under heaven was represented there in Jerusalem, and they *all* heard the "wonderful works of God" spoken in their own language (Acts 2:11).

The Holy Spirit gave the believers' words meaning. More than that, He gave their life new meaning! At sixteen, my life was transformed when I was baptized in the Holy Spirit. When that fire fell on me, there was no turning back. There was a new fervor, a new drive and passion to press forward, seeking more of Him. When the Holy Spirit comes, something changes in you, just as it did for the 120 in the Upper Room. Gifts are awakened, purpose is stirred and peace that comes only from the Comforter shelters you.

I have found that in my own life, it's impossible to function without the Holy Spirit's fire. Without His ignition, my words fall flat and empty. But how do you keep this fire burning?

First, I talk to the Holy Spirit. I think sometimes we forget that the Holy Spirit is a person! Frequently, I find myself talking to Him during my prayer time as I walk through our woods in Georgia. Many times, I sing to Him. There is nothing quite like true, undefiled worship to usher in the presence of the Holy Spirit. When Paul and Silas sang in prison, doors were opened, chains were loosened and prisoners were set free! If you're not musically inclined, maybe this makes you feel silly. Just remember that God is not interested in your talent, but in your heart. There is no perfect way to praise Him; the key is to thank Him for who He is and what He has done.

I want to challenge you to plug into the Power Source every morning. The power of the Holy Spirit is available to you, but you must be plugged in. Pray and ask God to fill, renew and empower you with His Spirit.

3. Get the right information.

What you take in determines what you see. If you get bad or frightening information, you'll see a world of fear and hopelessness. You can't listen to other people's opinions and hear God's truth about the situation. If you only focus on the negative news of the day, you'll miss God's word for today. What does the Lord say about your situation? That's the only information you need. God doesn't call you like you are; He calls you according to where you are going to be.

In Jeremiah 15:16 the prophet says, "Your words were found, and I ate them." It's not enough to hear the Word of the Lord. We need to hear it and receive it, let it get inside us. It doesn't matter what your circumstances are or what other people say. What does God say about your situation? What does God say about your family? What does God say about your future? What does God say about your freedom?

There's a remarkable story in the Old Testament about a man named Gideon who was hiding in a cave. God sent an angel to find him. The angel begins a conversation with Gideon by calling him a "mighty man of valor" (Judges 6:12). But Gideon didn't feel like one. He felt like a wimp. God told him in effect, *You're not a wimp. You're a winner. You're not a weakling; you're My man. You're the man of valor.*

What was God doing? God was putting the right information into Gideon. God wanted him to be aware of more than his fear and his overwhelming circumstances. And He wanted Gideon to get an image of himself as victorious. When you begin to believe and live out the truth, many times that right information will look like the opposite of what you are experiencing. Yet God is beginning to get you to understand that it's not about what you are; it's about what you will be.

The way to overcome what overwhelms you is to get a picture of yourself not as you see yourself, but as God sees you. God does not see you defeated. God does not see you bound. God does not see you as poor and broke. He does not see you as walked on and kicked by life. God sees you as an overcomer. God sees you as the head and not the tail. God sees you as blessed and highly favored.

> **God is beginning to get you to understand that it's not about what you are; it's about what you will be.**

God's way of bringing victory into your life is to show you yourself—not the way you see yourself, but the way He sees you. You may think you were, are and will always be depressed. You may see yourself as having to battle with yourself to get up every morning. You may picture your future as limited or as less than. But this is not what God sees. He has different information about you. He has the right information.

I love this Scripture:

> The Lord GOD has given Me the tongue of the learned, that I should know how to speak a word in season to him who is weary. He awakens Me morning by morning, He awakens My ear to hear as the learned.
>
> Isaiah 50:4

Every morning, God gives us a word. It's our job to listen and receive the word and get programmed right. What's the word? Read the Bible, the Word! It's not your feelings. It's not your situation. It's not what your best friend tells you or what your social media feed reads. The right information is that God will never leave you or forsake you, and that He has a great future for you.

I have disciplined myself to be in God's Word daily. Now, I know you may be thinking, *But you're a pastor, so it's your job!* Let me assure you that if I only studied to create messages, I would burn out. I study to fuel the flame that God has placed deep within me. I read His Word to know Him personally.

Does this mean that every day, I wake up overflowing with these things? Not always. But God has yet to fail me. It takes diligent effort on our part to keep the fire burning!

As we draw near to Him, He will draw near to us (see James 4:8). And when God is near to you, nothing can keep you from enduring.

4. Get in the right location.

I'm not talking about a physical location. In 1 Kings 17:2–6 there's a story about God telling Elijah to go to a certain brook. God had stationed ravens there to feed him since this happened during a time of famine. For three and a half years, God provided supernaturally for Elijah. But one day, the same voice sounded and told Elijah to pack up his belongings and go down to Zarephath, where God had told a widow to provide him with food (see verses 8–9). It was an act of faith for Elijah to leave the safety of his brook. But even as it was drying up because of the drought, God was already preparing other provision for him. The message is simple: If God is speaking to your heart to stay, stay. If He is speaking to your heart to move, move.

God is not going to do the same thing over and over in the same way. We have to be open to where or what God has for us. The first time the prophet Elijah saw his protégé, Elisha, Elisha was plowing in the field. Elijah passed him and threw his mantle on him, which was an ancient way of saying, "I have chosen you to follow in my footsteps. Let's go!"

Elisha was excited, but had a request: "Let me say good-bye to my parents first, and then I'll follow you" (see 1 Kings 19:20). What the young man ended up doing was going back to his field, killing his oxen and burning his plowing equipment to cook and serve the meat to the people. Then he came after Elijah.

The plow represented the security in Elisha's old life. His livestock and equipment were his livelihood. The plow also represented acceptance in the community's economy of farmers. Elisha was one of them. But before he could step into the destiny God had created for him, he had to break the plow.

Before I became a pastor at Free Chapel, Cherise and I were preaching all over the country. That was my plow. That was our provision, our security. It was making a nice living for my wife and me, and we loved every minute of it. But God had different plans for us. I felt in my spirit that He was telling me to break my plow, to stop trusting in my plans and accept the new thing He was doing.

You might be holding onto the old ways of doing things. God may be stirring something, even right now, within your soul, but something old might be stopping you from reaching forward into something new. Don't lean on what you used to do. Break the plow and allow God to show you a new way. Don't live in yesterday's expectation. Go or stay where God calls you.

5. Get the right focus.

Job 42:10 says that when Job prayed for his friends, his captivity was turned. Often in the process of enduring, our focus is wholly self-centered. We fixate on our needs, our problems, our prayers, our wants. Sometimes the best thing to do is to shift your attention off yourself and fix it on someone else.

Lend someone a hand. Ask friends what you can pray for them about. Share the Good News with a person who is struggling. Show a colleague you appreciate him or her by paying for a lunch together. Get out your wallet and donate to a good cause.

You have needs in your own life, but when you focus on the needs of others, everything changes. What you keep in your own hand shrinks, but what you put in God's hand multiplies.

6. Get the right timing.

The storm may come, but it can't last forever. The Bible tells us there is a time and a season to everything (see Ecclesiastes 3:1–8). Just as fall gives way to winter, winter to spring, and spring to summer, the sun is going to shine again.

I love how Psalm 37:34 reads in *The Living Bible*: "Don't be impatient for the Lord to act! Keep traveling steadily along his pathway and in due season he will honor you with every blessing."

> **All of God's promises have a time frame. He is not a right-now God; He is a right-time God.**

When a baby is incubated in his or her mother's womb, the baby stays there for a season. If the child comes too late, it could be dangerous. Same thing if he or she comes too early. But in due season, the child will be born.

All of God's promises have a time frame. He is not a right-now God; He is a right-time God. You need to know what time God's clock is on and get in sync with it.

The *PERMA* Plan

Dr. Martin Seligman is an American psychologist and pioneer in the field of positive psychology (a term coined by Abraham Maslow), which is a theory proven by scientific exploration. He also created a theory of well-being called *PERMA* that helps people flourish in life, regardless of negative situations or traumatic experiences. His theory of well-being includes five building blocks—Positive emotion, Engagement, Relationships, Meaning, and Accomplishments—that give you the hope you need to carry out your purpose in life. Today, many organizations across a variety of industries (including health care, education, corporations, government, professional sports and the military) use these principles as part of a larger training program to build resilience, well-being and optimism in individuals so they can navigate adversity and thrive every day.

Looking at these same principles from a biblical perspective, I'd like to show you how you can use these five building blocks to look ahead with joy instead of feeling discouraged by where you might be today. This is real, practical advice about how you can use the *PERMA* plan to help you carry out Step #3, *look ahead*.

P—Positive emotion

How do you approach difficulties and challenges? When you've reached a second or third setback, do you feel tempted to give up? What if you're called upon to be a part of an exciting, yet formidable project? Do you shrink back because of self-doubt or a perceived lack of experience? Do you use your time, talent and potential for good? Or do you allow excuses to rule your steps and keep you from your destiny?

I told this story in my book *Believe That You Can*, but I want to give you a short recap here since it illustrates my point about positivity so well. When Walt Disney was looking for someone to lead the design and construction of Disneyland Park in California, he felt Admiral Joe Fowler was the man for the job. Known as "Can-Do Joe," Fowler had a reputation for getting things done. He had served in the United States Navy during both World War I and World War II. Before his retirement in 1948, he designed and helped construct the USS *Lexington*, which served in the Battle of the Coral Sea, and the USS *Saratoga,* which participated in the Battle of Iwo Jima.[1]

Despite people's doubts that Fowler could actually construct and ready Disneyland for its grand opening in July 1955, he got it done. Following this incredible accomplishment, the retired admiral also served as general manager of the park's operations for years.

When he was 71, Fowler once again was asked to help bring another dream of Walt Disney's to life. Walt wanted to build an even bigger theme park in Florida. He convinced Fowler to oversee the design and construction of that park, too. Disney World opened in 1971, when Fowler was 77.[2] When he was in his eighties, Fowler was again asked to help with the design of the Epcot Center. He gave the familiar answer: "Yes!"

Fowler never met a challenge he couldn't face. Known in the Disney circle as having a positive response to any query that was presented, he met every demand with a smile and two words: "Can do!"[3]

No excuses! Fowler understood that excuses are the crutches of the uncommitted. He didn't lean on the negative. Fowler believed in his purpose and had the positivity required to get it done.

I like to say that we are always two or three sentences away from coming out of any setback. A lot of people who are struggling with looking ahead are saying things like these:

I can't.
I don't know how.
I'm not qualified.
I'm not smart enough.
This is impossible.

If that is you, instead, try flipping the script:

I can.
I'll try my best.
I'm going to learn how.
I'm knowledgeable and curious about new things.
With God all things are possible.

"The joy of the LORD is your strength" (Nehemiah 8:10). If you lose your joy, then you lose your strength. David wrote in Psalm 16:11, "You will show me the path of life; in Your presence is fullness of joy; at Your right hand are pleasures forevermore." David spoke of being at God's right hand, which in the ancient world was a symbol of being in favor with someone. David was telling us that the path of life is being in favor with God, because in His presence there is fullness of joy. The Hebrew word used in this verse for *fullness* is *soba*, which means to fill or to satisfy.[4] When the joy of the Lord becomes your strength, you replace the negative with the positive, and you will be able to conquer any obstacle that enters your path.

E—Engagement

At some point, you've got to get off the bench and get back in the game. You may not like where you are. You may be tired of the same old thing. You may feel crushed and defeated. But where you are is temporary, so get in the flow of working toward the future and looking ahead.

What can you do today to brighten someone else's day? How can you share the love of God with someone who is hurting? What can you do to take care of yourself physically?

Instead of being paralyzed by purposelessness, get up and start engaging in life. Press into your faith. Activate your will to believe, and keep going. Engage in the presence of God.

R—Relationships

Isolation is the enemy's favorite weapon. It is designed to cut you off from life-giving friends, family and community. People are in great danger when they continually isolate themselves. Isolation often leads to loneliness and depression. All good things in life flow through relationships. Ecclesiastes 4:9–12 talks about the value of friendship:

> Two are better than one, because they have a good reward for their labor. For if they fall, one will lift up his companion. But woe to him who is alone when he falls, for he has no one to help him up. Again, if two lie down together, they will keep warm; but how can one be warm alone? Though one may be overpowered by another, two can withstand him. And a threefold cord is not quickly broken.

Scripture also teaches that one can chase a thousand and two ten thousand (see Deuteronomy 32:30). Your authority increases when you engage your hope and faith with other people's. All it requires is two agreeing in order for anything to be done (see Matthew 18:19). Many great Bible heroes found their success by learning from and being encouraged by people whom God had placed into their lives. Things change when you maintain these types of power relationships with other believers.

Think about it this way: Somebody out there is already at the next level, where you need to be. Somebody else has already made it through the mess that you're struggling to get through. When you connect with such people, the power of God begins to flow in a new way in your life, and you find yourself moving from where you are to where you need to be. Be open and willing to learn as God uses relationships with other people to move you to a new level.

Do you have people in your life who lift you up, encourage you or help you on your journey? Is there someone who has successfully made it through the struggles you are facing? Do you have a godly mentor in your life? Ask God to reveal to you the people and relationships that will help you overcome. Link hands and hearts with others who will deposit faith in your spirit and not pull you back into the mud and mire of your past.

M—Meaning

A sense of purpose or meaning in our lives helps us look ahead instead of staying stuck where we are, or even going backward. In fact, having a mission can make all the difference, as this next story shows. I also told this story in *Believe That You Can*, but it bears repeating:

One winter day in Biloxi, Mississippi, a twenty-five-year-old woman decided to kill herself. She couldn't take it anymore and wanted her life to be over. She went to a bridge over the Mississippi River.

The water was frigid, and the bridge was high. She climbed over the railing and threw herself over. She hit the water with a terrible smack and started sinking.

Unbeknownst to her, a man on the bank of the river saw her jump. When he did not see her surface, he jumped in to rescue her.

She was sinking deeper when she heard him dive in. And then she started to hear this poor man flailing around. When he had jumped in, he had forgotten that he didn't know how to swim! This heroic idiot was splashing and screaming "Help! Help!" so the woman who was trying to kill herself swam to him and pulled him out onto the bank. He was choking, so she gave him mouth-to-mouth resuscitation. Somebody called 911, and both of them were taken to the hospital. Both of them survived.

I read about this in a news article, and the journalist who wrote up the story ended it with these words: "That night, it wasn't the man who saved her life. It was *purpose* that saved her life." Her purpose was to save the drowning man. Instantly, she had a mission. And having a mission saved her own life.[5]

You are going to need a mission to endure in this life. You don't have to be on a church staff to be a man on a mission or a woman on a warpath to defeat the enemy! You need to be motivated by a personal assignment. Maybe you have one, but you don't know what it is. God gives His people a dream, a mission for their lives that gives them meaning. It can be different things in different seasons, but He always has a purpose for you. If you don't know what your purpose is, ask Him for a vision of what He wants you to do.

What the enemy has used to harm you—the depression, the fear, the anxiety, the disappointments—can be used as fodder for your mission. Use the pain of what you have gone through to help bring healing to others. If you have battled depression, be a light for those in the darkness who can't see the road ahead.

A—Accomplishments

The Bible tells us we are more than conquerors through Christ (see Romans 8:37). By definition, a conqueror is one who is able to "acquire by force of arms; win in war; overcome by force; subdue; gain, win, or obtain by effort, personal appeal, etc.; gain a victory over; surmount; master; overcome."[6] Pretty impressive. You do realize that God says you are even *more* than that definition?

If a conqueror is a person who got out of a bad situation, a more-than-conqueror is a person who got out in order to go back in and turn that situation around. God may have freed you from anxiety or addiction, but He has even more in store for you than deliverance. He wants your life to tell His story.

What can you accomplish through God as a more-than-conqueror? I believe that what you have conquered is connected to the assignment God has given you to accomplish—to go back to the people who are in the condition you were once in and snatch them out of that hell-like existence.

Acting out of positive emotions, engaging in the life you've been given and connecting with the people in your life, you will experience a sense of meaning, and you will move forward in accomplishing God's purposes for you. You will endure and look ahead to a future that holds great promise.

Follow the Stones

There are times, however, that you have to look back to look ahead. God leaves us with lasting markers in this life that remind us to endure in the present so we can look forward to the future.

In February 1947, Douglas S. Mackiernan was a 33-year-old army meteorologist working in China. Out of nowhere, he made a strange career move and took an assignment at the U.S. State Department's most remote outpost, called Tihwa, a windy and rugged area in western China. Thing was, Mackiernan wasn't really a meteorologist. He was a spy for the CIA at his new post near the Soviet-Chinese border. Upon arrival in Tihwa, he spent hours each day transmitting encrypted messages and forming contacts with anti-communist White Russians. In August 1949, the State Department shut down the Tiwha consulate. All personnel were advised to leave the country immediately. Mackiernan, however, was told to stay behind to destroy cryptographic materials and monitor the situation. According to his wife, who spoke about it years later, it's possible that Mackiernan also wanted to remain on post to listen for the first possible Soviet atomic test.

Mackiernan and four others left a few days after everyone else. Their only route of escape was through dangerous terrain, taking them to India by way of Tibet. As they journeyed through the Himalayas, they came across some nomads who helped point the way toward India by telling Mackiernan and his crew to look for ancient cairns. A cairn is a pile of human-stacked stones that commemorate dead family members. People couldn't dig graves in the frozen ground for family members who died on the path. Instead, their bodies were covered with stones as a mark of respect and honor. Serving a second purpose, these cairns would then be used as geographical markers.

As Mackiernan passed each cairn, he was reminded that he was headed in the right direction. As long as he followed the stones, he would be on the right path that would lead to freedom. While he and his team ultimately made it to the border eight months after evacuating, in a tragic misunderstanding the Tibetan border guards began shooting at the group. Mackiernan and two others were killed. Only two men survived to tell the tale.

It's said that Mackiernan's body lies under a cairn of its own. His cairn joins a host of others that still help travelers find their own way in the frigid wilderness.[7]

Our lives are marked by loved ones and forerunners of the faith, too—generations who have gone before us and have left markers of their experiences to help us with our own experiences today. They may be gone now, but they have left us stones by which we can remember them and be encouraged to endure.

The book of Joshua gives us a powerful example of such sacred markers. After forty years of wandering, the time had come for the people of Israel to cross over into the Promised Land. Some four decades earlier, when the Red Sea had stood in their way after they fled from the Egyptians, God had intervened. He had parted the waters so His people could walk through on dry land. Once again, the people of Israel faced a similar predicament before they could enter the land of Canaan. Again God intervened, performing another miracle. He rolled back the waters of the Jordan River, just as He had done with the Red Sea before, and the people crossed over into the land He had promised them. Joshua explained to the people how they would use stones to commemorate this moment:

> "Cross over before the ark of the LORD your God into the midst of the Jordan, and each one of you take up a stone on his shoulder, according to the number of the tribes of the children of Israel, that this may be a sign among you when your children ask in time to come, saying, 'What do these stones mean to you?' Then you shall answer them that the waters of the Jordan were cut off before the ark of the

covenant of the LORD; when it crossed over the Jordan, the waters of the Jordan were cut off. And these stones shall be for a memorial to the children of Israel forever."

And the children of Israel did so, just as Joshua commanded, and took up twelve stones from the midst of the Jordan, as the LORD had spoken to Joshua, according to the number of the tribes of the children of Israel, and carried them over with them to the place where they lodged, and laid them down there. Then Joshua set up twelve stones in the midst of the Jordan, in the place where the feet of the priests who bore the ark of the covenant stood; and they are there to this day.

Joshua 4:5–9

God wanted the people of Israel to remember His provision and tell the story to their children, who would tell it to their children. He asked that twelve stones be brought to the other side from the riverbed so the people could forever remember what He had made possible. Future generations that would be discouraged and would need a boost to continue enduring in overwhelming times could look at those stones and say, "God did it once. He'll do it again."

What stones do you need to remember and follow? Maybe that of a praying grandmother? A neighbor who never gave up on you? A friend who believed in you more than you did? What stones can you look ahead to for the strength to push the vision forward and continue?

Maybe you didn't have the best examples to light your way. If that's the case, then you need to start stacking your own stones for your children and for those around you, because they will need some stones to follow.

There's a path that leads to righteousness, to life. You just have to follow the stones. When Jesus rose from the dead on the third day, He rolled the stone away from the entrance of the tomb to appear before His disciples. The stone is outside the empty tomb. Jesus is the living Stone. When you're tired, when your best-laid plans have fallen to pieces, when you have more questions than answers, follow the Stone that leads to life everlasting.

As weary travelers like Douglas S. Mackiernan know, sometimes the path forward is difficult to see. Sometimes when we look ahead, we see nothing but a storm of chaos. Sometimes we don't even have it in us to look ahead. But remember, what lies ahead is the promise that whoever "endures to the end will be saved" (Matthew 24:13).

LOOK AHEAD

These little troubles are getting us ready for an eternal glory that will make all our troubles seem like nothing.

2 CORINTHIANS 4:17 CEV

6

Step #4: Look Out

The ultimate attack of the enemy is to stop you from seeing the harvest that Jesus promised would come in the end times. In the words of Jesus, as natural disasters abound and societal conflicts rage, "this gospel of the kingdom will be preached in all the world as a witness to all the nations, and then the end will come" (Matthew 24:14). Satan wants nothing more than for you to stop caring about a lost and dying world. Yet this is one of the main visions God wants you to have in these overwhelming times. This echoes the Great Commission, the command Jesus gave after He rose from the dead and before He ascended into heaven: "Go into all the world and preach the gospel to every creature" (Mark 16:15). Those words are as true for us today as they were centuries ago.

Jesus didn't tell us to stay put or keep quiet. He expects us to go beyond the walls of our church community to share His message and love. The joy of living for Jesus is not just going to church and staying within the borders of our small group. It is when we get so full of the living water that we can't help but share our joy in the Gospel with others. How long has it been since you shared the Good

News with someone? May you continually pray that God gives you a desire to win the lost for Christ.

The fourth step you and I need to take as overcomers is to *look out*. You are not looking out for yourself. You are looking out for others. Our purpose in this life is not only to grow in our relationship with Jesus and be prepared when He returns. We must also reach the lost.

The Greatest Crime

While end-times experts don't agree on every detail about Christ's return, the alignment of nations or the Rapture, there is a consensus regarding an outpouring of the Holy Spirit that will result in an epic, end-time harvest of souls.

The responsibility of evangelism is entrusted to every believer. You included. Don't cringe too soon. I know for some, this evokes images of knocking on every door in your neighborhood and handing out tracts. Or stopping random people on city sidewalks or in suburban malls and initiating awkward conversations such as asking, "Do you believe in God? And if you don't, would you like to believe?" I realize these images of evangelism might make you feel weird. But this is not about being weird. It is about life or death.

The greatest crime on earth is not being committed by the usual suspects. It's not murderers, thieves or terrorists who are behind this atrocity. It's Christians who are guilty. It's a crime the Bible warns against, a crime that carries a heavy price. John 3:16 tells us, "For God so loved the world that He gave His only begotten Son, that whoever believes in Him should not perish but have everlasting life." If you don't believe in Jesus, you will perish for eternity in a place called hell. I know this is a heavy message, yet if you're tempted to close this book or move on to the next chapter, I invite you to stick with me anyway. Reading this might save a life—one or many. It is our responsibility to share the Gospel and help prevent people from perishing, help rescue the men and women who are on their way to death. When we shirk this responsibility, we commit a crime.

Consider this powerful passage found in the book of Proverbs:

> Deliver those who are drawn toward death, and hold back those stumbling to the slaughter. If you say, "Surely we did not know this," does not He who weighs the hearts consider it? He who keeps your soul, does He not know it? And will He not render to each man according to his deeds?
>
> Proverbs 24:11–12

There is an urgency attached to the Gospel. When we stay quiet, we are like the one who does not "hold back those stumbling to the slaughter." Our silence is the greatest crime we could ever commit. And it's one for which we will be held responsible.

I heard a story of a man who was condemned to die in the electric chair many years ago. On the day of his execution—in fact, minutes before he was strapped into the chair—the governor called the warden and granted the prisoner a stay of execution. Instead of understanding the weight of the message and moving forward with a sense of urgency, the warden took his time to relay the message. By the time he got to the execution room, it was too late. The prisoner had already been executed.

The message the warden received could have saved the prisoner's life, but the warden kept silent. I wonder how many of us keep silent instead of sharing the message of hope and everlasting life.

There are unbelievers who may never hear the truth of Jesus Christ if you and I do not bring it to them. When you share the hope of Christ, invite someone to church or tell another person about your faith, you're planting a seed in a moment that cannot be relived. God has placed you in that path for such a time as this and has entrusted you with His hope, His Word and His story. You never know what will lie on the other side of your obedience. Where would you be today if someone had not shared the Savior's story with you? We say we "follow" Jesus. But if we are not compelled to share His love, then it's time to reevaluate what we truly believe.

God expects more of us than trying to be good people. We must get a vision for souls. Winning souls to Jesus is serious business. It's not a suggestion or a nice idea. It's a command. I want to challenge and motivate you to share the Good News with others. This Good News is good for a reason. I'm confident that it has changed your life, brought you out of darkness, given you a reason to get out of bed in the morning and provided you with strength to face the day. Wouldn't you want to tell others of the Person who has transformed you for the better?

> **We say we "follow" Jesus. But if we are not compelled to share His love, then it's time to reevaluate what we truly believe.**

In our technologically advanced age, we are equipped with more ways than ever to reach people even in the most remote areas in the world. As of 2020, the Bible had been translated into more than 700 different languages, which means that over 5.7 billion people have access to the Bible in their native language. The American Bible Society plans to translate the Bible into all of the world's living languages by 2033.[1] Global evangelism is being encouraged, yet as Jesus said, "The harvest truly is great, but the laborers are few" (Luke 10:2).

I know it's easy to get caught up in the chaos and stresses of everyday life, because there are many. Yet we mustn't forget why we are here—to share what we have been given with others. Sense the urgency. As we started with in Step #1, first look within, and find in yourself that pressing need to win souls and save them from eternal death. Then look out, as this fourth step urges us to do, and identify those with whom you need to share the Good News.

There is more to being a Christian than just going to church to ask for our own answers to our own prayers. We must reach beyond the walls of our comfort and our preferences, and carry the message to others that Jesus loves them unconditionally, just as they are, and that He has a purpose for their lives.

Nighttime Heroes

God is looking for heroes in the nighttime hour of the Church today. Not heroes who wear capes or have superlatives in their name. But heroes who will do something for the Body of Christ selflessly, whether or not they feel anything is being done for them. Heroes who show up even when their service won't be seen or talked about.

When you're overtired or undervalued, overwhelmed or under-estimated, one of the most important things you can do is let God use you. God wants to use you in this hour. If ever there was a time to show up and bless the Body of Christ, it's now.

Being used of God for others might look a little different than you imagine. I want to introduce to you a man named Joseph of Arimathea, a New Testament man whom I call a hero in the night. This is what Scripture has to say about him:

> When the even was come, there came a rich man of Arimathaea, named Joseph, who also himself was Jesus' disciple: He went to Pilate, and begged the body of Jesus. Then Pilate commanded the body to be delivered. And when Joseph had taken the body, he wrapped it in a clean linen cloth, and laid it in his own new tomb, which he had hewn out in the rock: and he rolled a great stone to the door of the sepulchre, and departed.
>
> Matthew 27:57–60 KJV

This man Joseph was more than a spiritual figure in the community. He was a businessman, and a successful one. And using his influence and power, he went where no one else would go, to see Pilate. Joseph was a wise man who understood that he had been given wealth, prestige and power not for his own enjoyment, but for a purpose. Using his resources, Joseph begged Pilate for the crucified body of Jesus. In the nighttime hour, Joseph of Arimathea wanted to draw near to Christ.

Why does it matter that Joseph showed up at night? By nightfall, the show was over and everyone had gone home. Jesus was dead and seemingly had nothing to offer to Joseph. In this darkness, Christ was not performing miracles or raising the dead or opening the eyes of the blind or attracting tens of thousands of people just to hear Him teach. His body was scarred, marred and lifeless. He had no power, miracles or victory. Jesus was dead. He had nothing to offer Joseph.

Yet Joseph of Arimathea ministered to the body of Christ when it couldn't minister to him. This businessman stood with the Lord's body in the time of its transition. Look at it from this perspective, which is my interpretation: By offering what he had, Joseph helped position Jesus' body, which today is the New Testament Church, from a death position to being ready for a resurrection position. This one man used his influence, approached Pilate at night and begged for the body of Jesus. This is why I call him a nighttime hero. The disciples needed Joseph of Arimathea in that very dark hour. When the Church was powerless and had nothing to give, Joseph of Arimathea stepped up and gave all he had. Anybody can come to church when the Church is ministering to them, but how many come to the Church when the Church needs help? Joseph fought for the body of Christ. He believed in that body. He saw the potential of that body, and using what he had to rescue it, he ultimately begged for a role to play in positioning Jesus' body from death toward resurrection.

Just because you may be in a season of hardship and it may look as if the miracles and blessings have left, that is not the time to back off your commitment. This is when you can become a hero in the night. True heroes are the ones who do for others what they cannot do for themselves.

True heroes show up when no one else will. Joseph came to retrieve the body of Christ when no one else would. I wonder where Lazarus was, the man Jesus had brought back to life from the dead? Or where was the man whom Jesus had freed from thousands of demons? Or where was blind Bartimaeus, who could now see? Where were the crowds who had had no food, yet had been miraculously fed? Only one man came out of the shadows. Joseph didn't need the light of day so he could be seen and heard and applauded by others for his efforts. In fact, he used the cover of darkness to push his mission forward. I wonder how often we get so entrenched in our problems that we can't see farther than the tips of our own noses. And staying static, we sink deeper and deeper into the pool of discontentment. Heroes must be able to see beyond their own needs in order to meet the needs of others.

When we're willing to step out and do for someone in their night what they cannot do for us, we experience a transformation. We change from being consumers to being contributors. Instead of getting blessed, we become a blessing. Instead of begging for miracles, we become someone's miracle. Instead of always receiving, we position ourselves to give. And in these things, we stop taking and taking and taking, and start pouring life into the Body of Christ.

> **When we're willing to step out and do for someone in their night what they cannot do for us, we experience a transformation.**

Wanting nothing in return, Joseph of Arimathea came to Jesus' body when it seemed most helpless. To me, that is a hero. Can you take a minute and think of someone whom God used to be a hero in your night? Maybe it was the woman who wrote you the check that made up the difference in the rent you owed that month. Maybe it was the man who took time to pray with you when you crumbled at rock bottom. Maybe it was the person who let you borrow his or her car, or helped watch your children, or checked in on you every single day when your loved one passed away.

When is the last time you were a hero?

Everyone, every ministry, every believer, every church goes through a downtime, a period when our struggles outweigh our strength. The ones who run to us when we're on top of the world aren't the heroes. Heroes encircle us with love, compassion and prayers when all hell has broken through in our lives. When someone you know has relapsed, don't judge that person; reach out to him or her. Heroes help those who are down-and-out, even when others walk away. This is who the Church is supposed to be. We are not supposed to be the condemners of the world. A critical and judgmental spirit is dangerous. We are supposed to be heroes, believing that Jesus can save and change all of humankind.

As we grow closer to Christ's coming, we must participate in the work of God and the end-time harvest, which means looking out—outside our individual interests, to those who need Jesus.

Beyond These Walls

If ever there was a story in the Bible about looking out beyond yourself to others, it's the story of Joseph in the Old Testament (not to be confused with the New Testament's nighttime hero, Joseph of Arimathea).

The Old Testament's Joseph was blessed with a double portion blessing because, when it was in his power to do so, he decided that he would be a blessing to others. He didn't hoard his blessings, but abundantly gave what he had to others. No matter what others did or how they treated him, he was strengthened and blessed by God. Even though they had abused him, he blessed his brothers and Potiphar.

Because he extended blessing and reached beyond his own walls to them, so to speak, God blessed him doubly.

We see this blessing come on Joseph when Joseph's father, Jacob, was on his deathbed. Jacob began to lay hands on and prophesy over each of his twelve sons. When it was Joseph's turn, his father said this:

> Joseph is a fruitful bough, a fruitful bough by a well; his branches run over the wall. The archers have bitterly grieved him, shot at him and hated him. But his bow remained in strength, and the arms of his hands were made strong by the hands of the Mighty God of Jacob.
>
> Genesis 49:22–24

If you compare Joseph's blessing to his father's words over his brothers in the same chapter, you'll discover that Joseph's blessing runs at least five times longer. Why is that? It was because Joseph made a decision. He had a well, figuratively speaking, and instead of keeping all his well-watered growth to himself inside his own walls, he allowed the branches of his well-watered vineyard to spread beyond his walls.

Joseph's generosity was born out of difficult circumstances. He was the second youngest of twelve brothers born to Jacob. He was also his father's favorite, and everyone in the family knew it. Sold by his brothers, Joseph was purchased by Potiphar, an Egyptian official who served in Pharaoh's palace. Then he was falsely accused of rape by Potiphar's wife and thrown into prison. While in prison, he correctly interpreted the dreams of some fellow prisoners, and eventually he was summoned to interpret one of Pharaoh's dreams. Along with his interpretation, Joseph offered this Egyptian leader some good advice. Pharaoh was so moved by it that he appointed Joseph second-in-command over all of Egypt. Joseph was now a powerful man who held the keys to the world's food supply. And because Joseph wasn't concerned only about his own blessing, but also about the blessing of the people outside his own walls, God used him to help the Egyptians survive a seven-year famine. Joseph didn't keep the blessing of his garden inside the walls, so to speak. Instead, he reached out to meet the needs of others.

In reaching out, Joseph provided for his brothers, who had sold him into slavery. He provided for Potiphar's wife, who had falsely accused him. He provided for Potiphar, who threw him in jail even though he was innocent. Had it not been for Joseph, these people would have died in the famine. Joseph extended his blessing beyond his walls, beyond his confinement, beyond where he was. He cared about people who had nothing to offer him, people who didn't deserve his help, even people who had caused his past suffering. He shared his blessing with all of those in need.

This prophecy Jacob spoke over Joseph points us to Jesus Christ, the living water. When we find the living water, He changes our lives. Jesus turns our lives around and makes us new. He generously showers us with abundant blessing, so abundant that we will have more than we could ever use or require.

What do we do with that abundance? Are we sharing what we have with people beyond our own walls? Beyond these walls, people are lost and don't know that Jesus can rescue them. Beyond these walls, people are starving, thirsty and afraid. We walk among them every day, but we are often too caught up in our own lives to help them.

We have the living water. Now we must send a fruitful vine beyond our own walls and share what we have.

So many churches and so many Christians find the well of Jesus' love and forgiveness, but they just drink from it without ever reaching beyond their walls to offer it to others. It's time for all of us to get more concerned about sharing water from the well. In fact, when we start reaching out beyond our walls, God may decide to bless us double-portion style, as He did with the slave who turned second-in-command, Joseph. Remember that God blesses the generous spirit.

Jesus called us fishers of men (and women). I may not be a fishing guru, but I will tell you this: I don't care how beautiful or fancy a bass boat is, you will never see a fisherman go out on the lake and hang a sign that says *Fish are welcome here!* and expect fish to jump out of the lake and into the boat. It's not going to happen. So why do churches expect the lost to just wander inside their walls? If you want to catch fish, you have to get good bait.

That's why world missions is important. That's why authors invest time and resources in publications like the one you are reading right now. That's why television ministry is important. That's why we are present in the social media world, on TV, on the radio and have our website. It's different packaging to catch different kinds of fish.

I believe that God's Church can quench the thirst of a dying world. Let's be part of this generous irrigation effort. Like Joseph, look outward by letting the water flow outside your own walls.

Carry the Message

An 1899 essay by American writer and philosopher Elbert Hubbard is still passed around in military circles today to inspire initiative. In fact, years ago in some branches of the military, it was required reading. Hubbard's *A Message to Garcia* is a dramatized version of a real-life account of Army 1st Lt. Andrew S. Rowan's mission to carry a message from President William McKinley to General Calixto Garcia, commander of the rebel forces in eastern Cuba, at the start of the Spanish-American War. Rowan's story teaches us about fortitude, about doing what it takes to get things done.

In 1899, Spain still ruled Cuba. President McKinley wanted to recruit Cuban rebels to fight for the American cause, but there was no way of getting the message to General Garcia, who was deep in the jungle. The president of the United States had a problem, and Rowan was the problem solver. What made Rowan the man for the job was his willingness to accept this work without question. As Hubbard explains in his essay,

> McKinley gave Rowan a letter to be delivered to Garcia; Rowan took the letter and did not ask, "Where is he at?" By the Eternal! there is a man whose form should be cast in deathless bronze and the statue placed in every college of the land. It is not book-learning young men need, nor instruction about this and that, but a stiffening of the vertebrae which will cause them to be loyal to a trust, to act promptly, concentrate their energies: do the thing—"Carry a message to Garcia!"[2]

Rowan was tasked with an insurmountable assignment. He was to enter a hostile country and link two nations with one message. And Rowan said, "I'll do it." He echoed the words of Isaiah: "I heard the voice of the Lord, saying: 'Whom shall I send, and who will go for Us?' Then I said, 'Here am I! Send me'" (Isaiah 6:8).

Rowan didn't offer excuses. He didn't check his calendar. He didn't tell the president he'd do it next week. He didn't delegate the task to someone else. He didn't list reasons why it wasn't necessary. He didn't squirm his way out of the responsibility. He said, "Here I am! Send me." Rowan didn't know exactly how he was going to accomplish the assignment. He had one order and a lot more questions. But, through the rough seas, through mosquitoes and wild beasts, through jungles, through enemy gunfire, obstacles and adversity, he got the job done. Nothing was going to stop Rowan. Nothing was going to turn him back from his mission. He was determined to find and give Garcia the message.

The world needs more Rowans. God is looking for men and women, young and old, with initiative. He is looking for people who will go out and get it done. Jesus gave us the Great Commission in Mark 16:15: "Go into all the world and preach the gospel to every creature." If He told us to do this, there's a way to make it happen, if we will be faithful.

I know sharing the Gospel with others might seem intimidating to you.

But don't keep Jesus to yourself. Lives depend on it. Look out and reach out beyond your walls.

LOOK OUT

> But I tell you to look, and you will see that the fields are ripe and ready to harvest.
>
> JOHN 4:35 CEV

Step #5: Look Up

In Jesus' conversation with His disciples concerning the destruction of the Temple, we find our fifth step. Not only should we look out for others as the end approaches; we must also *look up*. Luke writes in his gospel,

> Now when these things begin to happen, look up and lift up your heads, because your redemption draws near.
>
> Luke 21:28

Did you catch that last bit of advice? "Look up and lift up your heads, because your redemption draws near." Jesus' last words on this topic of the end times are not words of doom and gloom. He may as well have told His disciples, "I don't want you to walk around depressed and defeated. You are not victims. Look up. Lift up your heads!"

When bad times strike, and as the reality of worsening enemy attacks increases the closer we get to the Second Coming of Jesus, we have a natural human tendency to look down. Stress weighs heavy on us and slumps our shoulders forward. Worry clouds our sight and destabilizes what should be a posture of strength.

Yet right in the middle of what seems like a fear-filled prophetic monologue depicting the image of the last days—replete with wars and rumors of wars, signs of natural disasters and a particular caution to pregnant women and nursing mothers—Jesus says the strangest thing: "Look up and lift your heads, because your redemption draws near."

Amid tumult and uncertainty, He encourages us to maintain a posture of looking up. It's a watchful and hopeful attitude—even joyful. We ought to have a look-up spirit.

Jesus gives us a reason for the hope: "because your redemption draws near." What does that mean? Before the end comes, God is going to send grace upon you and your loved ones. Many of the people whom you've longed to see get right with God will do so. Jesus is saying to you, *I'm not going to let the prayer and faith you have exercised over the years miss the target.*

This speaks of a ransom that the blood of Jesus Christ paid in full. The neighbor with whom you have walked through life's struggle, the spouse for whom you have spent years on your knees in prayer, the friend who gave up on God but whom you never gave up on . . . their redemption is drawing near.

We can look up because God made us promises and will not abandon our families until redemption, or grace, draws near to our house. Think back on the Sodom and Gomorrah story. God didn't rain judgment on that evil city until He released Lot and his family outside the city gates. God didn't shut the door of the ark until Noah and his family were safe inside, either.

Instead of fearing the world's huge dilemmas, it's time for us to look up. These problems and the troubles to come are just signs that we can look up and see the Word of the Lord coming to pass.

The same can be true when we're dealing with the everyday issues of life. Jesus told His followers that they would have trouble in this world—not just the end-times kind of trouble, but the kind of trouble that accompanies imperfect people living in an imperfect world every day. I know you're tired. I know you had trouble sleeping last night. I know you're wondering how you can juggle one more thing on top of the mountain-high pile of fine china you're already trying to balance in one hand. Remember the words of Jesus: "But be of good cheer, I have overcome the world" (John 16:33).

Refocus your gaze and look up.

The End Is Sure

Did you know that most movies are not filmed in chronological or script order? Some production teams may even shoot the final scene first. This is how God handles the story of your life. In Isaiah 46:10 God assures us that He is doing this: "Declaring the end from the beginning, and from ancient times things that are not yet done, saying, 'My counsel shall stand, and I will do all My pleasure.'"

God creates the ending of your life first. And in His story, you are an overcomer. This is already final. It is the finished product. It is who you are. This is the truth right from the beginning, even when your situation may look nothing like overcoming. Know that God's plan will not be frustrated—not by what you read in the headlines, not by a shortage of gas or toilet paper, not by the injustice of an evil that was done to you.

You are going to succeed because God has already determined your destiny.

Isaiah 46:10 makes reference to the omnipresence of God. He can be at all places, all the time. He's not just present in the room where you are sitting and reading this book; He is present with another individual reading this book on an island in the Philippines or on the coast of South Africa. Not only that, but God can be in your past, your present and your future at the same time. It's mind-blowing, isn't it?

Remember the shepherd boy turned king, David? After he had been anointed king, he still spent some time stepping around sheep dung before he had the opportunity to take the throne. God had called David to a greater purpose, even though he continued to care for bleating animals, carrying a staff instead of wearing a crown. Then when the giant and this young runt step up to do battle, it's obvious who's likely to win, right? Isn't it obvious? Yet when the prophet Samuel was pouring oil over David's head in ceremonial fashion, God was also pouring His protection over the young king-to-be. God was already going ahead of him in time, onto the bloodied battlefield where the odds, humanly speaking, were in Goliath's favor. David's victory was set. He would be king of Israel. He didn't have to worry about where he was in the moment and what it looked like, even on the battlefield.

"For I know the thoughts that I think toward you, saith the LORD, thoughts of peace, and not of evil, to give you an expected end" (Jeremiah 29:11 KJV). God had an expected end for David. And He has one for you, too.

God may not remove the Goliaths in our path, but His promise to give us an expected end will remain. What giant is blocking your vision, trying to keep you from looking up? Has your self-worth taken a beating? Has your depression spiked? Has your dream crashed and burned, making you not want to try again? I don't know how and I don't know what it will look like, but God will finish what He started. You were not born to stay overwhelmed forever. You were born to overcome.

Look up! God is going to get you to your expected end.

Look up! God is going to get you to your expected end.

The Bible lays out patterns and principles that show us the ways of God. What God did throughout His Word, He can do now. When it comes to trials, there are lessons to be learned. The Lord sets the times that trials start and determines when they end. If you read through the Bible, you'll notice the pattern that triumph follows trouble. Don't worry about the expiration date for your trials, but know that the Lord has already set the end date.

In Genesis 15 we see this particular pattern. In this passage of Scripture, God promises to make Abraham a great nation and give him and his descendants the land of Canaan. God actually makes Abraham stare at the midnight sky, plastered with millions of twinkling stars, and tells him, "So shall your descendants be" (verse 5).

From a biological perspective, this is a strange promise because Abraham did not have any children, and he and his wife, Sarah, were past childbearing years. But Abraham believes the promise, and the Bible tells us that God credits his faith as righteousness (see verse 6).

Yet there is even more to the promise. "Oh, heads up," God adds. And what comes next isn't the greatest news in the world. In fact, it sounds outright devastating:

> Know certainly that your descendants will be strangers in a land that is not theirs, and will serve them, and they will afflict them four hundred years. And also the nation whom they serve I will judge; afterward they shall come out with great possessions. Now as for you, you shall go to your fathers in peace; you shall be buried at a good old age. But in the fourth generation they shall return here.
>
> Genesis 15:13–16

Notice how God first gave Abraham a picture of the outcome— a nation with a number of descendants too great to count, given a land of promise. And then God told Abraham what would happen first. Three generations of these people would be in captivity. They would remain in bondage at the hands of their enemy. Yet there would come a day, God promised, where the people would be free and enter a land of their own.

While the people would be encountering trouble, God would have already established, over four hundred years earlier, a time limit for that trouble. It would not last a day or a minute longer than the time span God had determined. If He ordains a beginning, there is always an end. There is an expiration date for your trouble.

We see this pattern repeated in the story of Job. One day, God started bragging to Satan about how righteous Job was, saying in effect, "Devil, I found someone down on earth who trusts Me and loves Me and obeys Me" (see Genesis 1:6–12).

"Ha," Satan responded, "why wouldn't this man serve you? You've got a hedge of protection around him. He's in a perfect environment. He's got everything a man could want, and then some! You let me come around Job for a while and let's see how much he's for You."

And God gave Satan the power to destroy Job under one condition: The devil could not lay a hand on his actual life; he could not kill him. Job ended up losing his health, his children, his wealth, his possessions, his livelihood, his household—everything. We are reminded in Job that God will also set an end to darkness. God allowed the devil power over Job, but He put a limit on it and also brought the destruction to its expected end. And what did God do afterward? He blessed Job with double what he had before.

Lastly, we see this pattern evident in the life of Daniel. God told Daniel that Babylon would take the people of Israel into captivity, and there they would serve King Nebuchadnezzar. But He also told Daniel that after seventy years, they would come out and dwell in their own land, stronger than ever. God is in control, even over captivity. As He did for Daniel's Israel, He will bring you home.

Show Yourself Alive

Dark days don't last forever. Your sleepless nights won't continue for all time. Your toiling over the state of your relationship, the absence of a job, the stress of your child's illness—these will not forever encumber you. God sets limitations on trouble, and a day is already set for your freedom from captivity. In the meantime, you have a job to do. Your job is to show yourself alive.

Jesus foretold of His resurrection on numerous occasions. The second chapter of John records one such instance. After Jesus discovered the money changers and livestock merchants doing business in the Temple and drove them out, He was accosted by the Jewish leaders. They asked, in effect, "What right do You have to do this? If God gave You the authority, give us a sign to prove it!" (see John 2:18).

Jesus gave them an answer they didn't expect or understand: "Destroy this temple, and in three days I will raise it up" (verse 19).

What a ludicrous response! these Jewish leaders thought. *Who is this man, saying that this Temple that has taken 46 years to build can be destroyed and raised up in three days?*

But Jesus, as He often did, was speaking in a parable. He wasn't referring to the actual Temple that stood before them. He was talking about His body. He knew the day would come when He would be beaten and crucified. But resurrection always follows death. This is the pattern that Jesus started and left for us to follow. On the heels of His announcement of death came the Good News that He would be raised up to life.

But first, Jesus would endure a tribulation like no other. When He was betrayed by His own disciple, Judas, and arrested in the Garden of Gethsemane, Jesus turned to the priests and the captain of the Temple guard who had come to take Him away and said, "When I was with you daily in the temple, you did not try to seize Me. But this is your hour, and the power of darkness" (Luke 22:53). The time had come. It was the enemy's hour. Jesus allowed it to happen because He knew there was an expected end.

He would be whipped, battered and abused. It would look as though the end had come. Breath would finally leave Him. He would be pierced on His side one last time, before He was peeled off the cross. He would be dressed in graveclothes and placed in a tomb that was sealed with a large stone. It would appear on all counts that death had conquered Jesus.

I love the fact that after Jesus was crucified, Scripture says that He showed Himself alive (see Acts 1:3). He didn't just show up. He wanted to show people that He had made it. That He was still standing. That He was and is victorious. That death does not have the final word, and He is alive.

> If you're in a situation beyond your control that is taking what feels like the best of you, God wants you to show yourself alive.

If you're in a situation beyond your control that is taking what feels like the best of you, God wants you to show yourself alive. Job showed himself alive after he had shed the tears, asked God the questions and broken like pieces of pottery, his laughter gone. And after Job admitted feeling alone, acknowledging that he couldn't see God in any direction, he said these powerful words: "But He knows the way that I take; when He has tested me, I shall come forth as gold" (Job 23:10).

The devil tried to wear Job out, just as he's doing to us today. Dreams fade. Relationships shatter. Promises fail. Economies collapse. Jobs are cut. Losses abound. But in spite of trial after tribulation after pain, we can praise God. We can pray. We can trust and believe. We can focus on what matters: Jesus. This is how we show ourselves alive.

Show yourself alive by bursting out in praise and worship instead of speaking words of negativity. Don't berate or pity yourself because you are weak in your present circumstance. Recognize the truth that you are anointed.

Arguably the greatest sporting event of the twentieth century, with one billion people watching around the world, was the boxing match between legends Muhammad Ali and George Foreman. This historic athletic event, known as the "Rumble in the Jungle," took place in Kinshasa, Zaire, on October 30, 1974. Ali was a 4–1 underdog. Foreman was an undefeated champion and ten years younger.

Born Cassius Clay Jr., Ali was nicknamed by the media, among other monikers, the "Louisville Lip" because he was born in Louisville, Kentucky, and he never stopped talking. The iconic boxer was a loudmouth who taunted his opponents any chance he could. Before a fight with British boxer Henry Cooper, he said, "Henry, this is no jive. The fight will end in five." He spouted one of his most famous lines, "Float like a butterfly, sting like a bee" to Sonny Liston. And of course, he would often repeat perhaps the most well-known self-proclaimed title of all: "I am the greatest."

Before meeting Foreman on the canvas, Ali quipped to the press, "How much longer do we have to wait? I'm ready to whup George Foreman right now."[1] Ali fought with his hands and with his words.

Despite his brazen confidence, Ali was not favored to win the match. To most, Foreman was invincible, indestructible and unbeatable. He took the first round, as expected. Ali changed his tactics in round 2. In a strategy he called "rope-a-dope," Ali leaned on the ropes and covered up while Foreman punched him continuously on his arms and body. If you were watching the scene and didn't know Ali's plan, it looked as if Foreman were crushing Ali. Blow after blow. Punch after punch. Thing was, none of the blows landed solidly enough to hurt Ali. They did, however, tire out Foreman, which was Ali's plan all along. By the seventh round, Foreman's energy was beginning to get zapped. When Foreman hit Ali hard to the jaw, Ali whispered in Foreman's ear, "That all you got, George?" And in that moment, in Foreman's words, "I realised that this ain't what I thought it was."[2]

By the eighth round, all the wild shots Foreman had thrown had depleted him of strength. Ali threw a five-punch combination, ending with a left hook and a hard right to the face that brought Foreman straight to the canvas. Seconds later, to the shock of one billion people, Foreman was clearly down for the count and Ali was officially declared the winner.

What has the enemy hit you with? Depression? Disappointment? Dysfunction? Show yourself alive. The devil may have thought he was going to knock you out, but I believe all he can do is knock you down to your knees. You don't have to stay there! As Paul wrote to the early believers, "We are hard-pressed on every side, yet not crushed; we are perplexed, but not in despair; persecuted, but not forsaken; struck down, but not destroyed" (2 Corinthians 4:8–9).

Do you have the courage to stand up to the enemy and whisper in his ear, *Is this all you got?* You can, because you are more than a conqueror (see Romans 8:37).

Eagerly Awaiting . . .

In Christ, you will one day show yourself alive eternally. But until that glorious end arrives, we must learn to do something that sounds contradictory, something both passive and active. We must learn how to fight—and how to wait—at the same time.

Waiting is part of the human experience. According to various studies,

- Americans will spend a total average of 43 days over their lifetime being put on hold by customer service.[3]
- The average American commuter will spend 54 extra hours a year in traffic delays (extra meaning the time spent driving at congested traffic speeds rather than non-traffic speeds).[4]
- The average person will spend 10 years standing in line over their lifetime.[5]
- A survey in Great Britain reports that Brits spend an average of 6.7 years of their lives just waiting around, whether in queues, on hold, for their children, or for the kettle to boil.[6]

Waiting is something every one of us has to do. Often, our waiting feels pointless at best and miserable at worst. But as Christians, our waiting is purposeful. We wait for the day when our prayers will be answered, the reconciliation will come, the seed we have planted will take root and bring forth fruit, and the grief will cease. In both our striving to want better and out of our desire to live a life of purpose, we will always remain in a waiting game of sorts.

Within a few months after Paul planted a church in Thessalonica, he wrote a letter to the believers there to encourage them, telling them,

> For from you the word of the Lord has sounded forth, not only in Macedonia and Achaia, but also in every place. Your faith toward God has gone out, so that we do not need to say anything. For they them-selves declare . . . how you turned to God from idols to serve the living and true God, and to wait for His Son from heaven, whom He raised from the dead, even Jesus who delivers us from the wrath to come.
>
> 1 Thessalonians 1:8–10

Paul made the powerful statement that everyone was talking about the Church of Thessalonica and how they were waiting for the return of Jesus. Their testimony didn't just include getting saved, baptized, turning from idols and sharing with others the Good News. Their transformation included what they were looking forward to: the Second Coming of Jesus Christ. They fully expected His return. And they were waiting for it.

They weren't the only ones waiting in this sense. Scripture also tells us that everything God has made in creation—the stars, the moon, the sun, the earth, the trees, the plants, the flowers—all of it is eagerly waiting:

> For we know that the whole creation groans and labors with birth pangs together until now. Not only that, but we also who have the

firstfruits of the Spirit, even we ourselves groan within ourselves, eagerly waiting for the adoption, the redemption of our body. For we were saved in this hope, but hope that is seen is not hope; for why does one still hope for what he sees? But if we hope for what we do not see, we eagerly wait for it with perseverance.

Romans 8:22–25

Notice the groaning and birth pains mentioned in this passage. One could consider natural disasters like earthquakes, floods and tsunamis as wailing songs that the earth cries out in agony, part of being cursed since Adam and Eve sinned in the Garden. As beautiful as some parts of the world are, our world is still under the curse. Every flower, every snowcapped mountaintop, every trout-filled babbling brook, alpine meadow and rugged red rock cliff may be a breathtaking wonder, but they are nowhere nearly as breathtaking as they will be when the curse is lifted and their natural wonder goes on full display. In the meantime, we wait.

We, and the whole of creation, eagerly await Jesus' return, and await the Rapture, which I'll address in the next and final part of this book (particularly in chapter 9). We await the day when our broken bodies will be redeemed into perfection. Inside the soul of every believer should be a sense of homesickness. We should long for the soon return of Jesus Christ. The book of Hebrews uses similar poetic language to address this languishing: "And as it is appointed for men to die once, but after this the judgment, so Christ was offered once to bear the sins of many. To those who eagerly wait for Him He will appear a second time, apart from sin, for salvation" (Hebrews 9:27–28).

The state of mind of every believer needs to be the eager expectation of the Second Coming of Jesus. We need to be turbo-energized by that thought. Are you ready for His coming? Are you eager for His coming? Are you yearning for His coming? You can love life on earth. There is nothing wrong with living with purpose and enjoying your life. But you also must remember that this earth is our secondary citizenship. Our primary residence lies in a place somewhere beyond the clouds.

Philippians 3:20 says, "For our citizenship is in heaven, from which we also eagerly wait for the Savior, the Lord Jesus Christ." There is that phrase again: "eagerly wait." Notice the pattern! Whatever you are waiting to experience on this earth is nothing compared to the joys and pleasures that await you on the other side. To be eager in this way, we must cultivate our imagination about what lies in store for us in heaven.

Heaven is a real place. The path to heaven is one road, and it's narrow. It has one door, and that door is Jesus. It has dimensions and cities and housing. We will trade our sick, tired, abused bodies for glorified ones. There is no death in heaven, and there are no tears. No disappointment, no sorrow, no temptation, no evil. Can you imagine what it's going to be like? One hundred trillion times greater if you get to heaven than all the glory and money combined that this world has to offer. The least in the Kingdom of heaven will receive greater than those who think they have a lot of stuff on earth. What kind of reward? "No eye has seen, no ear has heard and no one's heart has imagined all the things that God has prepared for those who love him" (1 Corinthians 2:9 CJB).

The Church needs to be eagerly awaiting the Son of God. We have to get the fire in our walk. We have to get that "eagerly awaiting" spirit. We have to get sanctified. We have to get filled with the Spirit. It's time to start living today in the power of the Holy Spirit, and in much assurance in our Gospel!

Bill Borden was born in the late 1880s, the heir to a million-dollar family fortune. Today, the Borden company is worth $2 billion. When Bill graduated from high school, his parents gifted him with a trip around the world. While visiting Asia and Europe, he felt called to be a missionary. A friend commented that if that was what Bill chose to do, he would be wasting his life. It is said that in response, Bill wrote two words in his Bible: *No reserves.*

Bill enrolled in Yale University to learn languages and prepare for life abroad, and he started a prayer group that morphed into a movement. What started as 150 students his freshman year grew to 1,000 students by his senior year. Bill also used his family fortune to give to people in need in the community, and he could often be found sharing the Gospel with students on campus, as well as with people off campus. When he graduated, he refused high-paying job offers and wrote two more words in the back of his Bible: *No retreats.*

Bill felt called to preach the Gospel to Muslim people groups in western China. He set sail toward China, stopping first in Egypt to study Arabic. While in Egypt, however, he became ill with spinal meningitis. He died a month later, at the age of 25. Prior to his death, the story goes that he wrote two more words in his Bible: *No regrets.*

This is the kind of eagerness that I want to characterize our waiting. *No reserves. No retreats. No regrets.* We can wait with this kind of intensity and urgency because we know Jesus is coming back one day. He shows Himself alive and shows you that your glorious ending is also certain.

And what now? In light of His return, how should we live? We live eagerly waiting His return, with confidence and anticipation. We live with joy and with hope. We share with others His faithfulness and His goodness that we have seen in our own lives.

LOOK UP

To those who eagerly wait for Him He will appear a second time, apart from sin, for salvation.

HEBREWS 9:28

PART III

GET UP, GET OUT, GET FREE

The closer we get to the Second Coming, the stronger the enemy's assaults against us. The first time the devil came on the scene, he arrived in the form of a serpent. Hundreds of years later, when the apostle Peter wrote about him, he described the devil as a roaring lion. By the time the book of Revelation was penned, the enemy was referred to as a dragon. Note the progression.

Today, we're fighting an enemy with more brawn, scathing wit and stamina than mere venom, razor-sharp claws and fiery breath; we're dealing with the spirit of the Antichrist. In this third part of the book, I pull back the curtain on a group of manipulating spirits that are attacking the Body of Christ. They come from the dark spiritual legacy of one of the most wicked people who ever lived: Jezebel. These forces are determined, yet they are also already defeated—overwhelmed by the cross, the blood of Christ and the power of His resurrection.

As we will talk about more in these remaining chapters, you and I were not born to be defeated. We will encounter problems this side of eternity, but God has destined us as overcomers. We can overcome the enemy's assaults. We can get up, get out and get free, because ultimately, we were born to win.

The Overwhelming

Jezebel, a cruel queen and ruthless murderer, may have lived thousands of years ago, but her manipulative and deadly tactics are very much alive today through her "spiritual children." Before I tell you about them and the things that they attempt to do, I want to look at a little background on Jezebel herself.

Let's pause for a second first, however. If the name *Jezebel* is throwing you off and you're really hoping this book is *not* a misogynistic witch hunt looking to judge a certain type of woman, you can breathe easy. It's nothing like that. In fact, don't get hung up on her gender. The spirit of Jezebel is an equal opportunity spirit. It can operate within both men and women, young and old.

Jezebel's legacy is mentioned three times in the Bible. First, 1 Kings 18 relates this wicked queen's massacre of the prophets of the Lord. Second, Matthew 14 talks about Queen Herodias, her spiritual descendant, who manipulated the death of John the Baptist. Third, Revelation 2:20 mentions "that woman Jezebel," another daughter of this spirit, in the letter written to the Church at Thyatira. In this last Scripture, the spirit of Jezebel is shown as one of the predominant spirits that will attack the Church in the end times. And as I write these words, that invasion is currently underway.

An Ancient Spirit

Here's where the invasion began. Jezebel ruled as queen of Israel, along with her husband, King Ahab, from 874–853 BC. She was a tyrant who worshiped multiple false gods and decimated anyone who opposed her, including the prophets of Israel. When Jezebel turned her attention to the prophet Elijah, he became so afraid that he fled and found refuge in a cave. There, overcome with such despair, he begged God to let him die.

Jezebel's reign ended in her death. Elijah's successor, Elisha, witnessed her end as she was thrown out a window and trampled by a horse. Then her lifeless body was eaten by a pack of wild dogs and was unidentifiable after that. All that remained was her skull, her feet and the palms of her hands (see 2 Kings 9:30–37).

Queen Jezebel was quite dead in a physical sense, but her legacy continued across the generations that followed, and in fact continues to this day. We see it in action in Jesus' day, when the gospel author Luke wrote about how John the Baptist, in the spirit of Elijah, arrived on the scene to announce the coming of Jesus (see Luke 1:13–17). What happens to John as the forerunner of Christ? The spirit of Jezebel attacks him!

John the Baptist had called out King Herod for marrying his brother's wife, and the outraged king had thrown him in jail. The king's wife was so embarrassed at the open rebuke of sexual immorality that she conspired against John. During her husband's birthday feast, she arranged for her daughter to dance a provocative number before the king and his guests. Herod was so entranced that when the girl took her final bow, he jumped to his feet and exclaimed, "I'll give you whatever you want, up to half of my kingdom!

Anything at all!" The girl didn't ask for a Tesla chariot or a Louis Vuitton satchel or a courtyard apartment. She asked for what her mother advised: "Tell the king you want the head of John the Baptist" (see Mark 6:14–29).

This is a biblical instance of Jezebel's spirit at work. We don't wage war against flesh and blood. We battle with unseen enemies like this wicked spirit.

> **We don't wage war against flesh and blood. We battle with unseen enemies.**

Approximately a thousand years after Queen Jezebel died, the book of Revelation was written. This prophetic work launches with letters addressed to seven churches. In these passages, Jesus describes characteristics, good and bad, that illustrate what the Church will look like during the end times. Some of these churches are lavished with compliments. Others are called out for their despicable behavior. Some are both applauded and admonished.

In Revelation 2:19–28, addressing the Church of Thyatira (labeled in some translations as the "Corrupt Church"), Jesus actually mentions the offspring of this wicked queen:

> I know your works, love, service, faith, and your patience; and as for your works, the last are more than the first. Nevertheless I have a few things against you, because you allow that woman Jezebel, who calls herself a prophetess, to teach and seduce My servants to commit sexual immorality and eat things sacrificed to idols. And I gave her time to repent of her sexual immorality, and she did not repent. Indeed I will cast her into a sickbed, and those who commit adultery with her into great tribulation, unless they repent of their deeds. I will kill her children with death, and all the churches shall know that I am He who searches the minds and hearts. And I will give to each one of you according to your works.
>
> Now to you I say, and to the rest in Thyatira, as many as do not have this doctrine, who have not known the depths of Satan, as they

say, I will put on you no other burden. But hold fast what you have till I come. And he who overcomes, and keeps My works until the end, to him I will give power over the nations—

> "He shall rule them with a rod of iron;
> They shall be dashed to pieces like the potter's vessels"—

as I also have received from My Father; and I will give him the morning star.

This text serves as a warning to us today that even though Jezebel has been dead for almost three millennia, her spirit is very much alive.

Purpose Killers

You may or may not have given much thought to Jezebel's wicked kids before now. Yet every single day, they fight to manipulate your heart and mind. Just as Queen Jezebel brought depression and discouragement to Elijah, the same is happening to the Body of Christ today. Her spiritual children strive to entice and enslave you. They long to see you quit. They work night and day to torment you and keep you from fulfilling the purpose God has for you. And to rob you of peace.

Who are Jezebel's kids? They are these tormenting and manipulative spirits:

- Fear
- Discouragement
- Depression
- Lust

In the rest of this book, I'm going to expose how the enemy is using these spirits to try to keep you and me from overcoming whatever is trying to overwhelm us. I'll also arm you with a battle plan destined to help you win. These pages will equip you with the knowledge you need to be on alert, and with biblical stories and confessions you can use to overcome when it feels as if you are overwhelmed. God's Word will work if you work it!

As you read the pages ahead, know that I am not glorifying the problems the enemy is magnifying in these end times. I am giving you an opportunity to be on high alert. Much of what Jesus taught indicates that these predominant spirits will try to influence our thinking, our emotions and our heart, soul and mind. The moment you shed light on these spirits and drag them out of the darkness of your own struggle's privacy into the light of God's Word, you begin to overcome.

God's Word will work if you work it!

The evidence of Jezebel's wicked legacy at work is all around. That legacy is chilling. We see it in the fact that suicide is the second leading cause of death among individuals between the ages of 10 and 34. It's reported that around the world in 2019, 1 in every 100 deaths was by suicide.[1] Suicide is the fourth leading cause of death globally, ahead of road injury, tuberculosis and interpersonal violence.[2]

We see this spirit ravaging almost a quarter of the U.S. population alone through anxiety disorders, the most common mental illness in America.[3] This spirit also dominates men and women addicted to pornography and is trying to snuff the life out of the 4.8 million people trapped by or forced into sexual exploitation.[4]

Let's get personal. The effects of Jezebel's legacy can keep us up at night with panic attacks and fear of the future. Chaining us to addictions and unhealthy dependencies, her children can paralyze us from forward movement. They can even manipulate us in small ways, like when we spend more time running through what-if scenarios in our head instead of submitting our worries to God, or when we allow negativity to dominate our thought life.

Fear, discouragement, depression and lust may show up in different ways, but they have a united motive: to hinder the children of God from what they are called to do and who they were created to become.

Recognizing this is especially important right now, as we approach the Second Coming of Jesus. The enemy is on high alert because he knows he doesn't have much time. He will use any means necessary to hinder your spiritual growth, distract you from what's most important and use fear or other unruly emotions to keep you as far away as possible from living to your fullest potential.

But wait! God hasn't left us unarmed and hopeless.

Though the enemy seeks to destroy, his intentions alone don't guarantee an accomplished mission. Let's not forget how Jesus ended the letter in Revelation 2: "But hold fast what you have till I come. And he who overcomes, and keeps My works until the end, to him I will give power over the nations" (verses 25–26).

If you're struggling in any of these four areas, you can have authority over this Jezebel spirit and her wicked children. Incredible victory can flood your life. But first, it's time to kill the legacy. Cut it off at the roots. Jesus uses strong language when it comes to these spirits. "Kill their influence—completely cut it out of your life," He says in effect, because He knows they will kill you.

You have to stop these spirits from operating in your life in their embryo stage, because if you let them grow and you feed and shelter them, they will captivate your heart, destroy your mind and turn you away from everything good in your life.

Whether you are suffering in silence or out loud from these overwhelming spirits of fear, discouragement, depression or lust, God has not left you alone to fight the enemy and his hordes that try to overwhelm you.

There's power in the blood of Jesus—enough power for you to overcome.

Face Fear with Faith

While I was writing this book, I tested positive for COVID-19. I had all the symptoms of the disease. I experienced aches, chills, headache, a loss of taste and a high fever. As miserable as those symptoms were, what seemed worse than the virus was my fear of it. Every cough, every ache, every spike in temperature triggered dread that I was getting worse. I remember the incessant questions that kept me up at night: *It's hard to breathe. Should I go to the hospital? Will I need a ventilator? Am I going to make it?*

The fear was real. I had been quarantined alone for several days. There were times when I would wake up in the middle of the night and my mind would race down the road of negative possibilities. I thought of every worst-case scenario you can imagine. There's a part of me that is embarrassed even to tell you this. I mean, I'm a pastor! I'm supposed to be a pro at battling fear, right?

Wrong. Whether you're a pastor or not, we all wrestle with fear. My fear of COVID-19 was a moment of crisis that forced me to make a decision. In moments like that, we must all decide whose report we will believe.

Get Your Mind Right

We find this important question in Isaiah 53:1: "Who has believed our report? And to whom has the arm of the LORD been revealed?" In other words, what's the state of your belief system? Is it steady and stable, resting on the promises of God no matter the circumstance? Or does it teeter, depending on how you feel in the moment? Are you quick to turn up the volume on negative what-if questions and worst-case scenarios, as I did during those midnight hours when I was stricken with COVID-19?

As you read through this book and become more aware of the signs of the times, determine on what or whom you will set your mind. If you're not careful, you can become trapped into paying more attention to the bad reports than to what God says. The key to overcoming in overwhelming times is to renew your mind by feeding on a diet of prayer, worship and meditation on God's Word.

> The key to overcoming in overwhelming times is to renew your mind by feeding on a diet of prayer, worship and meditation on God's Word.

The commandment the Bible gives most often is "fear not," and it's typically coupled with God's promise "for I am with you." If you allow it, however, fear will stop you from fulfilling the assignment, the mission, the purpose and the dream God has put you on this planet to accomplish. But if you plug into the power of the One who helps us overcome fear, you will see the greater truth that "God has not given us the spirit of fear, but of power and of love and of a sound mind" (2 Timothy 1:7). Power, love and a sound mind come from one source: faith.

In overwhelming times, one thing is certain: You're going to live either by faith or by fear. No matter what we see going on around us, we need to close our eyes and listen with our hearts. We need to choose to see the greater truth of God's presence. For we walk by faith, not by sight.

Much Ado about Nothing

Mark 5:21–43 tells the story of a twelve-year-old girl, the daughter of a temple leader, who died from an unknown cause. When Jesus came into the house where she lay, an uproar of grief surrounded Him. The eyes of the girl's family and loved ones were swollen with tears. Wails of mourning echoed throughout the house. Sobs of denial broke out from mourners with trembling shoulders. When Jesus observed the scene, He said something strange: "Why make this commotion and weep? The child is not dead, but sleeping" (verse 39).

In the King James Version, He says it like this: "Why make ye this ado, and weep?" *Ado* is not a word most of us use in modern vernacular, although Shakespeare made it famous in a play he wrote that was first performed in 1612, titled *Much Ado About Nothing*. The Greek Word for *ado* in the verse is *thorubeo*, the root of which means "to be in tumult, i.e., Disturb, clamor—make ado (a noise), trouble self, set on an uproar."[1]

Jesus asked this girl's family, "Why are you making so much ado about this situation?" Before I continue, I absolutely must underscore that Jesus was not downplaying the tragedy. He was not minimizing their grief. He was not treating the little girl's death lightly. He was saying that, even in the darkest moments, even when the fear that death has won is present, tangible and suffocating, there is still a choice to make: fear or faith. And in His peculiar statement, He was telling the mourners to choose faith.

The circumstance was grave, but when compared to the One who was in the room, it was much ado about nothing. We need to get that word deep down in our spirit. No matter what comes our way, we do not need to freak out, panic or take things into our own hands. Instead, we can speak back to the enemy and tell him, "You're making much ado about nothing!"

I am in no way minimizing whatever it is you are facing, either. Fear is real. What role does fear play in your life? Would you consider yourself a warrior or a worrier? Being a warrior doesn't mean you never feel afraid, of course. Being a warrior means that when fear threatens to engulf your mind, you declare faith over that feeling and experience God's nearness to you in that time.

Facing Fear

In 2020, the most googled phobia was *anthropophobia*, a big word that means the fear of other people. I'm sure this had a lot to do with the COVID-19 pandemic. Anthropophobia comprised 22 percent of all fears searched in the United States, five times more than that same fear was searched in 2019.[2] New York's most searched phobia? The fear of being alone. California? The fear of social media. Georgia? The outside. I can't say I understand that one.

Most of us suffer from more than one fear. We may be afraid of speaking in public and also of not having enough money for retirement. Or maybe we are afraid of needles and also that God won't hear our prayers. Whether we're afraid of flying or dying, most of us can probably say that we've been bombarded by a spirit of fear, sometimes to the point that we are paralyzed or neutralized from taking a step forward in life, never mind fulfilling the purpose God has called us to fulfill.

Let's get personal. Fear is a constant battle with me. I don't know why God uses me sometimes, because I truly am the epitome of 1 Corinthians 1:27, the Scripture that says, "But God has chosen the foolish things of the world to put to shame the wise, and God has chosen the weak things of the world to put to shame the things which are mighty." My fear might make me weak, but I know that God who is in me is greater than all my fears.

This may sound crazy, considering I've been preaching for almost a handful of decades, but I have never gotten completely used to speaking in public. I'm definitely not as nervous as I was when I started out, because I've learned how to control the anxiety. But I know what it's like to live with waves of panic that swell over you with so much force that it feels as if you can hardly breathe.

Anytime you embark on a God-ordained mission, the enemy will release a spirit of fear against you. The fear you feel bubbles up like a shaken can of soda, ready to erupt. And that fear takes on dread, or what the Bible calls evil foreboding (see Proverbs 15:15 AMPC). Our worries multiply and swell into something greater, a negative expectation that becomes all consuming.

Much ado about nothing? It sure doesn't feel like that, right? But feelings and truth are two separate things. When Jesus is in the room and He reminds us of His presence, fear has no place. No matter what comes our way, we need to remind ourselves that faith is what overcomes fear.

Fear dominated much of the years 2020 and 2021 because of a very real pandemic. Many lives were lost. That's real, and that hurts! What's just as true is that over the last two centuries, life expectancy in the United States has more than doubled, to almost eighty years. In America, we're actually living longer than at any time in human history. This is also true in many other countries globally.[3] Our times are in God's hands. Jesus has the keys of hell and death, so what keys does Satan still have? None! He doesn't even have the keys to his own kingdom anymore. Jesus openly subdued the devil and his minions, and God gave Jesus all rule and authority in this age and in the age to come. The Kingdom of heaven knows it. The kingdom of darkness knows it. The problem is, too many Christians don't live as if they know it, so they are not operating from that position of victory. God holds the keys to life and death!

My brother Richie passed away in December 2012. I had the privilege one time of taking him to the doctor. He was in the final stages of fighting against cancer and was thin and sick. Just he and I were in the car. It was obvious to Richie, and to his wife and kids, that unless God intervened, at the age of 54 he would be going home soon to be with the Lord. In fact, at his final appointment the doctor had told him that he had a few weeks, a month at best, to live. Richie and I were close and could talk about anything. But the day I took him to the doctor, I didn't want to talk about the elephant in the room—death. I could tell Richie wanted to talk about it. He kept starting and stopping his sentences, until finally he broke it open. "Jent," he said, "unless God performs a miracle, I know I'm going to die."

I'll never forget what I asked him next. I was scared to ask, but I could sense that he needed to talk about it. "What's that like?" I asked. "What are you feeling? Are you afraid?"

"I am absolutely not afraid to die," he replied. "I just hate that I'm not going to be there for my wife and children. I don't want my wife to carry the burden of raising a family alone."

Richie never gave in to a state of dread. He refused to be tormented over the inevitable. And while he struggled with fears for his loved ones who would remain on earth after him, he didn't let the enemy do all the talking. He prayed. He worshiped. He read the Bible out loud. He fought fear with faith.

When you turn on the news, or when you scroll through social media and fear that you're missing out—staring at photos that showcase perfect families, idyllic vacations or fancy parties you're not invited to attend—you're going to need to choose faith. Speak over that feeling of dread. Remind yourself that God is for you, that He is with you, that He is holding you in the palm of His hand.

Faith is not denial. It is not false hope that pretends you don't have issues, problems or situations that require emergency intervention. This is why so many people haven't seen a doctor in years. They're afraid to hear what the doctor would have to say. This is fear talking! I love saying that everything is better with Jesus, including trouble. Face and battle fear with faith. Don't deny what is happening in or around you. Confront the fear and focus on God.

As my brother Richie learned to do, we need to stop letting the enemy do all the talking. Sometimes, it's the fearful whisperings of our own imagination that we need to take captive. Imagine all the fears that bombard people day in and day out: *My daughter just started driving, I wonder when her first car wreck will be. What if I can't have any more babies? Oh, he's never going to marry me. I don't want to know what the biopsy is going to say. What if treatment doesn't work? What if I get fired? What if I can't cut it? What if I get promoted and they find out I'm not that good? What if he stops loving me? What if she finds out what the real me is like?*

I could fill volumes on all the fears that occupy the space in our minds. Sometimes, we just have to stop and shut fear up. If you can't hear anything above the decibel level of your fears, whip out the Bible and start reading. This is not going to remove the emotion of fear from your life, but it will help weaken its power over you.

Feel It, but Don't Act on It

The enemy is masterful at making us afraid of what could happen. I think about Queen Jezebel and how Elijah had to overcome fear. The Bible tells us that the prophet had called the king, the queen and the nation of Israel to repent, but that the two leaders refused. In a dramatic showdown battle with false gods, Elijah called down fire from heaven, which consumed the altar he had built and drenched with water. After that display of God's power, Elijah then ordered the killing of 450 prophets of Baal (see 1 Kings 18).

This enraged the queen. She swore to kill Elijah, and he fled into the wilderness, finding refuge under a juniper tree. "I can't take it," he cried. "Just take my life," he begged God (see 1 Kings 19:4). Then an angel came down from heaven and fed the prophet. Notice that Scripture doesn't say anything super spiritual about Elijah's situation, but rather that the angel cared for his physical needs: "Chill out. Take a nap. I'll come back with a snack. First things first."

This might sound extreme, but it was an extreme situation. We're talking about a prophet who had just, through the power of God, killed 450 prophets of Baal. And now he wanted to die himself because he feared a ruthless queen. Forty days and forty nights passed. And as Elijah summoned physical and spiritual strength, he got up and out from under the juniper tree and soon went back to the palace. This time, he was not afraid. In a prophetic warning, he told the king, "Thus says the LORD: 'In the place where dogs licked the blood of Naboth, dogs shall lick your blood, even yours'" (1 Kings 21:19).

> Compared to God, whatever enemy or problem you are facing, I promise you it is much ado about nothing.

In the natural Elijah was afraid, and rightfully so. But something kicked in. Compared to God, Jezebel was much ado about nothing. Compared to God, whatever enemy or problem you are facing, I promise you it is much ado about nothing. Don't allow fear to dominate your life. Act in faith first.

Faith fights feelings. You don't need to feel a certain way to exercise faith and keep believing, even when you're afraid of what tomorrow holds, when you fear the promise won't come to pass, or when you're terrified because you don't know if your child will make it through the night. Faith says, *No matter what I feel, God is here. He is real. He is alive. And I won't let my feelings stop me from believing in and praising Him!*

Imagine how Noah must have felt on that boat on the 39th day of rain, with every animal God ever created and only one window. And as the giant ship was rocking day after day, night after night, up and down on ceaseless waves, Noah must have been battling nausea and doubt. But guess what—he stayed faithful to God on that boat. He may not have felt so hot, but he hung onto the promise of dry land, no matter how bad or frustrated he may have felt.

And Job? The man who lost everything, including his children, his business, his home, his money, his livestock? Imagine the roller coaster of feelings he must have ridden. Anger and grief and despair eating up every inch of sanity and hope he had left. He didn't know why God had allowed such tragedy, yet one thing he did know—that his Redeemer lives and that God is the one who gives and takes away, bless His name.

The irony in Christianity is that even when we do not feel strong, we are strong. We are told that God's grace is made perfect in our weakness (see 2 Corinthians 12:9). Do you understand that even when you are scared to death, you are a giant? Even when you are trembling at the foe you are facing, greater is He that is in you than he that is in the world!

Don't act on your feelings. Don't allow them to determine the direction of your day, your mood or the choices you make. Choose to activate your faith by praying, worshiping, praising and reading the Bible. Affirm the Word of God in your spirit. Don't repeat or agree with the whispers of fear in your mind; affirm what God says.

The stage is set for the drama of the ages to unfold. While chaos will be the new norm, God's people can choose to live with steadfast hope in a shaky world. Make a decision today to live by faith over feelings.

Fear of End-Time Uncertainties

One of these days, in the morning, noon or at midnight, without warning, like a thief in the night Jesus Christ will suddenly appear.

Millions of Christians will disappear from their homes, businesses, schools and offices. People of all ages, races and walks of life will suddenly vanish. Conversations will be interrupted mid-sentence. One person will be taken, while others will be left behind. Families will be eating a meal at a table when suddenly a portion of their members will be taken, while the rest will be left behind. Cars empty of their drivers will crash on the freeways, airplanes will crash in fields, babies will be missing in cribs and children will vanish from schools. Fear will run rampant as the same anxious question is asked over and over in the homes, streets and factories where people have disappeared into thin air: "Where has everyone gone?!"

The whole world will enter a state of hysteria as people see television clips, hear radio reports and read online stories announcing that tens of millions of people have vanished. Cries of weeping will fill the air in every city and community. Stadiums will be closed, and restaurants will seem empty. Businesses will be paralyzed, the wheels of industry will come to a screeching halt, many important government and military positions will be left vacant. The whole world's economy and infrastructure will begin to collapse.

Mass communication will shut down and power grids will fail as the world falls into pandemonium. People will panic, not believing what they are seeing or hearing. They will search frantically for their missing relatives and companions who are gone, only to come to the realization that the missing are nowhere to be found. Jesus Christ has come again. The world's panic and shock will be just the opportunity Satan has been waiting for.

What I have just described is not the opening scene of a movie. It's a description of the Rapture of the Church. There is so much we do not know, details that are yet to be revealed. But from what I have researched and studied, along with other theologians and scholars, here's a bird's eye view of what's to come: The Antichrist, Satan incarnate, will move in, and with him will come the seven-year tribulation. The first half of this period will include unprecedented prosperity. Peace like the world has never known. The hungry will be fed, the homeless will find shelter and the poor will have means. Wars will cease. Unity will reign. The Antichrist will establish a league and covenant between the Arab nations and Israel. He will rule from the city of Jerusalem and will set up his own government.

When those three and a half years are over, however, the Antichrist will turn in character and allegiance. He will demand that all the people of the earth worship him. Not only that, but the Bible says that he will defy God in heaven, and he will defy all the people on the earth who love God. All kinds of judgment will fall on the earth, and the peace that was once cast will be destroyed.

At the end of the seven-year period, the battle of Armageddon will unfold. The world will unite against Israel and will gather to fight in the Valley of Megiddo. This will be an even bigger underdog scenario than David going up against Goliath. As Israel is on the verge of being annihilated, fighting for her life with every last bit of strength, Jesus will return. He will set His foot down on the Mount of Olives and supernaturally intervene on behalf of the nation of Israel. And with Him will come all those who were raptured seven years earlier (see Zechariah 14:4–5, where this final outcome of the battle is foretold).

When you read this summarized account of the last days I just provided, I'm sure it may trigger fear. You might just find this to be the ultimate battle between fear and faith. But here is some encouragement in light of what can be considered fearful times: When Paul talked about the Second Coming of Christ in 1 Thessalonians 4:13–18, he didn't end his explanation of the event by telling his readers to start popping antianxiety pills, cross their fingers and hope for the best. "Comfort one another," he wrote (verse 18).

In other words, this time can bring us together in unity, to comfort one another with the hope that we have beyond all these events. Our hope is not in politics, science or mankind. Our hope is in the certainty of Jesus Christ's Second Coming. We don't know the exact time of His return, but Jesus was born on time, died on time, rose from the dead on time, and He's coming back the second time on time. God has everything under control. Don't be hit by headline hysteria. Don't be dismayed by tales of gloom and doom.

God's people are not to be anxious or upset. In a dark world, we are to have hope.

Faith as the Ultimate Fear Fighter

The Bible tells us, "Fight the good fight of faith, lay hold on eternal life, to which you were also called and have confessed the good confession in the presence of many witnesses" (1 Timothy 6:12).

That's a bold command. When I read it for the first time, I couldn't quite figure out what was so "good" about a fight. I'd never been in a good fight before; I'd always been the one who got hit. But you know why the Bible calls the fight of faith good? Because we know who wins. God does!

Faith has never lost a battle. If you fight fear in your own power, with your own will and your own self-discipline, you will worry yourself to trembling pieces. But if you begin to activate your faith, your faith will battle and conquer fear, and the pressures of life will not overcome you! Oh, the pressures will come and will try to crush your spirit, but they will not win.

Think of faith as the "white corpuscles" of your spiritual anatomy. In the physical, these white blood cells are an important part of your body's natural defense system because they are the cells that engulf bacteria and disease. In the spiritual, fear is like an infection attacking your spirit. Faith will rise up like a white corpuscle and defend you against this attack.

Fear will put to death the promises of God. Faith, on the other hand, will bring life. Remember the woman with the issue of blood who reached out to touch Jesus, confident that simply touching the hem of His garment would make her well? An act of faith in her life brought her a miracle (see Mark 5:24–34).

I also imagine the conversation that Mary Magdalene, Mary the mother of James, and Salome could have had with neighbors who had heard they were on their way to anoint the dead body of Jesus after His crucifixion:

"How are you going to anoint the body? The tomb is blocked by a stone!"

"We're not sure. But we're going anyway."

"But there's a Roman seal on the tomb. You'll get in trouble if it's broken!"

"That's true. But we're still going to anoint His body."

"But there are guards there!"

"I hear you. Still going. Now leave us be!"

And when these three faith-filled women arrived at the tomb, it was empty. Jesus was alive (see Mark 16:1–7). In other words, faith produces life in what seems dead in us. Because of their faith, the women found life where death had been! Fear produces distrust in the promises of God. Allow your faith to fight your fears, and receive the living Jesus, who gives you the promise!

Faith also fights facts. Facts don't lie, but faith can overcome the facts. It was a fact that Goliath was favored to win his fight with young David, but only faith could make a teenager throw the right rock at the right place at the right time. It may have been a fact that Abraham and Sarah were well past their childbearing years, but faith made it possible for them to plan their baby shower and welcome their baby boy into the world. Facts say that water can't support the weight of an adult male (or any other human being), but somehow Peter walked on the sea. I could go on. Just writing this is activating my own faith!

One thing I've noticed is that the sayings we have as humans look very different in God's language. For instance, when we're about to run a race or do something significant, we might say something like, "Ready, get set, go!" But God puts it this way: "Go, get set, ready!" I was not ready when God called me to get married. I was twenty-five, and marriage scared me to death. That was a fact. Cherise was only eighteen. But God's timing was not our timing, and here we are today. I was not ready to pastor this church when the time came. I thought it was too soon. I thought I was too young. I didn't think anyone would respect me. But God said, *Go, get set, and I'll make you ready. I don't call the qualified; I qualify the called.*

Faith will fight for our future. For the believer, tomorrow is not a leap into the dark. If you have faith, no matter where you are right now, you don't have to be afraid of the future. Although uncertainty seems the most certain of truths, remember what Jesus said when the disciples questioned Him about the end of days. We talked in chapter 7 about how, after He addressed the signs of the times and the destruction of Jerusalem's Temple—stuff that would make even the bravest soul tremble in fear—He closed with this: "Now when these things begin to happen, look up and lift up your heads, because your redemption draws near" (Luke 21:28).

From what I hear and what I see on social media, end-time anxiety is at an all-time high. Are we close? Does the intense political and racial divide in America mean we're on the brink of a civil war? Whether you're buried in reading about vaccine conspiracy theories or are trying to figure out if you'll get married before Jesus comes back, here's a word from God to you: *Look up! Lift your head!*

Wherever God has you or is leading you, know that fear is not part of that equation. The finger of God never points where the hand of God doesn't provide! Fear not death. Fear not devils. Fear not disease. Fear not calamity. Fear not the end of the age. Why? Because Christ is Immanuel. And Immanuel means three things:

1) He is God in us.

2) He is God with us.

3) He is God for us.

God is in the business of helping us overcome our fears. When you choose to be a warrior over a worrier, you become an overcomer in His Kingdom. Will you live in fear or faith?

The choice is yours.

10

Dismantling Discouragement

There is no question that God plants dreams inside the heart of every person. A dream is a God-given destiny. It could be something God is calling you to do or to be, something that He has given you the innate skill, talent and opportunity to carry out. It could be a vision you have for your marriage, for your family, for your workplace, for your neighbors or for your community.

But along the way, something has happened. Hell's nightmares are always nipping at the heels of God's dreams. You have no doubt felt the nightmarish discouragement—the closed doors, the rejections, the financial turmoil, the sickness, the lack of growth.

Unless you can endure hell's nightmare, you will never experience heaven's dream for your life.

I found that the moment most people give up is also the moment of greatest opportunity. Everything you want is on the other side of not giving up. Believe it or not, the nightmare is the pathway to your destiny because it purifies your motives and tests your character. Trouble is your pathway to triumph. Your pain is your pathway to giving God higher praise. Your mess is your pathway to the miraculous things of God in your life.

The closer you get to fulfilling your purpose, the tougher it gets. It's like a woman who, longing to be a mother, becomes pregnant. She's carrying around this dream of motherhood and enjoying the ride. But when the time comes to give birth, that dream is only born through an experience of excruciating pain.

Calvary was the pathway to the dream of the Church. God said, *I have a dream. I want a Church*. Jesus said, *I'll build My Church, and the gates of hell will not prevail against it*. And hell's forces said, *We don't think so. We'll stop You. We'll nail You to a cross*. But when Jesus stepped out of that tomb, guess what? The nightmare became the pathway to the dream.

If you're battling the spirit of discouragement today and you're hearing voices telling you to give up, I want to remind you that whatever dream God has birthed in your life, He has promised He will complete it. Philippians 1:6 tells us so: "He who has begun a good work in you will complete it."

Pick Up Your Dropped Dreams

You may know the Old Testament story about Abraham and Sarah having a son named Isaac. But prior to Isaac, Abraham had another son named Ishmael. While this couple was waiting on their promised son, Sarah decided that she couldn't wait any longer. She encouraged Abraham to sleep with her maid servant, Hagar. Abraham agreed, and Abraham and Hagar produced a son named Ishmael. But in time, Isaac was born to Abraham and Sarah. Ishmael was not the chosen son.

Sarah regretted her earlier actions and demanded that Abraham kick Hagar and Ishmael out of their house. In Genesis 21, we find Abraham collecting food and water for these two and sending them on their way. As Hagar and her son wandered through the wilderness of Beersheba, their water ran out. So did their food. Without any reserves, and being scorched by the sun, mother and son faced death. With no strength left, Hagar placed her barely conscious boy under a dead shrub and walked away, wailing. She couldn't bear to watch what she knew was going to happen to him. "Let me not see the death of the boy," Hagar cried (verse 16).

In what was probably the worst moment of her life, Hagar dropped her dream. Wandering in a wilderness without food, water or resources, in a moment of utter discouragement, she left her son to die and walked away because she was too heartbroken to witness him suffering. But something amazing happened: "God heard the voice of the lad" (verse 17).

If you have a God-given dream, that dream can cry out to God like Ishmael's voice, even if you've given up on it. God heard Hagar's lost dream, and the grieving woman heard from heaven, "What ails you, Hagar? Fear not, for God has heard the voice of the lad where he is. Arise, lift up the lad and hold him with your hand, for I will make him a great nation" (verses 17–18). God delights in restoring our dreams to us.

> **If God planted a dream in your heart, no matter what it looks like right now or where you may have dropped it, it's time to pick it back up. Dust it off and place it back in God's hands.**

If you are enduring a nightmare, the time is coming when you will experience the dream's restoration. Discouragement may have overwhelmed you to the point of giving up and quitting on what you once believed God promised you. But He is not through with you yet.

If God planted a dream in your heart, no matter what it looks like right now or where you may have dropped it, it's time to pick it back up. Dust it off and place it back in God's hands.

We All Get Discouraged

In the opening scene of *It's a Wonderful Life*, we see a succession of houses and we hear the prayers being offered by their occupants:

I owe everything to George Bailey. Help him, dear Father.

Joseph, Jesus and Mary, help my friend, Mr. Bailey.

Help my son, George, tonight.

The plethora of prayers from George Bailey's friends and family reach up to heaven and catch the attention of two angels named Joseph and Franklin. They decide to send a novice angel, Clarence, down to earth to help a man named George Bailey. Joseph sends for Clarence, who asks what's wrong with this man: "Is he sick?"

"No, worse," Franklin replies. "He's discouraged. At exactly 10:45 p.m. Earth time, that man will be thinking seriously of throwing away God's greatest gift."[1]

This gift the angel refers to is George Bailey's life. This man's despair illustrates how total and destructive discouragement can be.

Remember how Elijah asked God to take his life after Queen Jezebel threatened to kill him? That's what discouragement can do; it causes you to throw away your potential and God's purpose for your life. If you don't fight the spirit of discouragement, it will halt your progress. You will lose the courage required to step out, take risks and try. The spirit of discouragement will threaten to bring you down.

Perhaps your discouragement right now comes from a pandemic that canceled your dream. Or discouragement may come when you pray for something and it seems you wait a lifetime without an answer. You may feel discouraged enough to give up after you receive yet another rejection or another denial. When you do all the right things and suffer, while others seem to prosper without a struggle, it doesn't take long for discouragement to set in.

Don't be embarrassed or ashamed if you feel discouraged. Discouragement hits the best of us. John the Baptist reached a point when he was devastated, not only because he had just been thrown into prison, but because he wanted Jesus to assure him that he was doing the right thing. Like so many of us, John just wanted to see that his efforts were not in vain. This is the same John who had an up-close and personal relationship with Jesus, the one who had proclaimed of Jesus: "Behold! The Lamb of God who takes away the sin of the world!" (John 1:29). John had a personal revelation of the Messiah, yet toward the end of his life he felt abandoned and plagued with doubt. He sent a message to Jesus asking, "Are You the Coming One, or do we look for another?" (Matthew 11:3). In other words, John wondered, *Did I imagine all these things? Did they really happen? Have I gotten myself sucked into a case of mistaken identity? Is Jesus really the One?*

Discouragement will cause you to question what you previously affirmed about your faith in God. John was so discouraged that because of it, he entertained the thought of looking somewhere other than to Jesus for his hope. When you're tempted to pull away from Jesus because He's not working like you want Him to work, you're in danger of being overwhelmed by discouragement. Discouragement will fast-track you back where you don't belong—back to the binges, the consumption, the illicit sex, the likes on social media—whatever makes you temporarily feel better, whatever gives you the dopamine high or numbs the ache of wanting to call it quits.

To combat discouragement, we must first learn a lesson about time: God's time is bigger than ours. If we want to overcome this child of Jezebel, discouragement, we must learn to wait.

Learn to Wait

As long as the earth exists, the Bible tells us, there will be seasons: first sowing seed time, then waiting for growth time, then finally the harvest (see Genesis 8:22). We cannot forget the time in between the seed and the harvest. To reap that harvest, we must learn to wait. As Scripture says, "for in due season we shall reap if we do not lose heart" (Galatians 6:9). You can't get the fruit before it's ripe. God sent His Son only when the fullness of time had come (see Galatians 4:4).

A cactus called the queen of the night looks like a dead bush until it's time to bloom. For one night out of the entire year, it blossoms with white flowers up to eight inches wide. We're talking 364 days of waiting for one bloom. Every seven years, white and purple flowers bloom from the ten-foot-tall giant Himalayan lily. In these plants, we see the kind of patience required to witness the blossoming of something beautiful.

Waiting with patience is not instinctual for most people. What are you waiting for today that causes your stomach to tighten into a knot of anxiety? What have you lost passion for because it hasn't happened the way you wanted? What prayers have gone unanswered for so long that you have isolated yourself and crawled deeper into the cave of discouragement?

Have you ever owned a one-of-a-kind item that was made especially for you? Maybe it was a bracelet or a journal with your name on it. I want you to start thinking of waiting as a custom-designed, just-for-you storm, created to bring you one step closer to your destiny. Remember Jonah, the prophet whom God called to preach to the city of Nineveh, but who ran away instead and ended up being swallowed whole by a whale? Jonah's story teaches us about the Master Designer behind our seasons of waiting and what He has customized for us.

Jonah 1:17 says, "Now the LORD had prepared a great fish to swallow Jonah." Then, a few chapters later, we read that "the LORD God prepared a plant and made it come up over Jonah, that it might be shade for his head to deliver him from his misery" (Jonah 4:6). In the next verse, the Bible tells us that God prepares one more thing for Jonah, this time a worm. Think about the time all these preparations must have required. God must have started designing the plant to grow big enough for Jonah to live under before He had ever gotten Jonah into the fish, and even before Jonah had encountered the storm where he would be thrown overboard.

The next time you want to hurry up, get through and get out of the storm, consider that God has not forgotten you. He is busy designing events that will yield blessings in your life. Wait and see.

When our kids were little, Cherise and I decided to take them fishing. Each child had his or her own little fishing pole, and I helped each one get a live worm on the hook for bait. (Well, actually Cherise was better at baiting the hooks than I was.) The kids were excited at this new game, in awe of the squirmy worms and ready to toss their fishing lines into the lake and pull up a largemouth bass. But five minutes after our lines hit the water, the novelty wore off. The kids started groaning and complaining: "This is taking too long!" "I'm so bored!" "When is something going to happen?"

I had an idea. I told one of my daughters I'd hold her fishing rod while she went over to Mom to get something for me. In her absence, I caught a fish, took it off my pole and hooked it onto hers. "Look, honey," I told her when she returned, "there's something on the line!"

That little girl's scream just about busted my eardrum. "Oh my gosh! I got one! I got one!" Lo and behold, when she pulled out her line, there was a fish dangling on the end of it. She looked at me, her eyes glowing with pride, and exclaimed, "I did it! I did it, Daddy!"

If you are in a holding zone and it's feeling boring or overwhelming, or if you're on the verge of quitting, remember that God is doing something beneath the surface. Your Father is putting a fish on your hook. He is holding you in the palm of His hand. He is saying, *My grace is sufficient for you.* And He's got a lot more coming in your life if you won't give up!

When God is doing something big in your life, you can't rush it. Sometimes the best miracles take time.

The Blessing in the Breaking

Not only do some miracles take longer than we'd like, but they also often come by way of strange means. Often, our breakthrough will come out of our brokenness. To combat discouragement, reframe how you see even the most discouraging of circumstances.

The story of the feeding of the five thousand is recorded in all four gospels. We looked at it in chapter 4, but let's return to it again for a moment. Jesus was teaching a crowd in Bethsaida that numbered five thousand, not including women and children. It was getting dark when the disciples suggested that Jesus send the crowd away so the people could go home while it was still light and get some food and rest. But Jesus had another suggestion: He told His disciples to feed the crowd instead. The only food the disciples could find was one boy's lunch of five loaves of bread and two fish. To Jesus, this was more than enough. He took the food, blessed it, broke it and gave it to the disciples to start passing out.

It's interesting to note that as Jesus was praying over the food, the quantity was still five loaves of bread and two fish. Nothing had changed. It was only after He broke the meal and started distributing it among the crowd that the food multiplied. Then Jesus and the disciples began to lose count of how much food there was. Every man, woman and child had eaten, and there were twelve baskets full of leftovers in addition.

The breakings of life produce the blessings of life. This is a spiritual law.

Jesus fed the multitude through the breaking process. The breakings of life produce the blessings of life. This is a spiritual law.

When you felt discouraged in your season of brokenness, God wasn't trying to crush you. He was getting ready to bless you. Blessings come after the rejection, the betrayal, the disappointment and the loss. It may not seem to add up, but the greatest blessings come out of the hardest breakings. The very thing you're cursing is the very thing God is going to use to multiply and bless your life.

Now, here's the thing. God is a good chef, and He is also good at math. He's even got a book in the Bible called Numbers. When the people of Israel wandered in the desert for forty years, God provided for them from the bakeries of heaven. Every morning when they got up, there was the manna that God had prepared for them. Since He is not a God of waste, He made just enough manna for one day. No leftovers. It's a great lesson for us today—to depend on God one day at a time.

Then sometimes God offers another lesson: abundance. When God cooks, He knows how many people He's cooking for. So when the bellies of the crowd began to rumble, Jesus knew how much food they would need to be satisfied. He could have been precise. He could have broken off just enough to feed five thousand (plus those women and children) and stopped there. He knew when He got to enough for the last person who needed a meal, but He purposely designed it so that there would be leftovers. He kept on breaking off more than enough. He chose to give them overflow.

Don't you ever let people tell you that God just wants to give you enough. That sounds really religious when people say it. But God doesn't just want to give you enough. God's name is *El Shaddai*, not *El Cheapo*. In Hebrew, *El Shaddai* means more than enough.[2] He is a God of overflow. He doesn't just want to give you enough; He wants to give you more than enough.

I want you to understand today that God's blessing is greater than our capacity to contain it. It is not limited to what your cup or mine says we can hold. When He blesses what has been broken, it will be pressed down, shaken together and running over.

Being broken hurts. It feels as if you can't breathe. The walls close in on you. You can't find even an inch of hope. Like Elijah, you may even want to lie under a tree and die. Or like Jonah, who did the same sort of thing. I want you to know that what you are going through today is the very thing God will use to bring the blessing.

Encourage Someone Else

Do you remember when Elijah heard that Queen Jezebel had put a hit on his life, and he ran into the wilderness? As he lay there in despair, God sent provision by way of an angel to feed him. God was strengthening him for the journey ahead. Elijah found a cave and planted himself inside. He continued his self-defeating diatribe and begged God to let him die. You know what God told him to do? Get out of that place and go anoint three people (see 1 Kings 19:15–16).

If you are desperate to come out of a cave of discouragement, go encourage someone else. When was the last time you shared hope with someone? Or prayed for them in their hour of need? When was the last time you blessed someone else instead of expecting a blessing of your own?

God knew that as long as Elijah was focused on himself and his discouragement, he wasn't going to be encouraged. The shift would come when he was willing to share his anointing with others. Whenever I have felt discouraged but have preached from the heart, sharing with others the anointing God has given me, some of the best sermons have come.

Think about someone today you can check in on. Whom can you take out to lunch? When you share your anointing, God will bring you out of your cave of discouragement.

Hard Places Lead to High Places

You may have received or believed a promise from God, but that promise is taking much longer and sucking strength, power and even faith out of you. God may have told you that you are on your way to a higher place, but right now you are stuck in a hard place. You're in between the promise and the provision. Maybe you're so tired that you're willing to forget the promise and move on. Perhaps you think God has changed His mind, and that's why He seems silent or why you feel that He's so far away.

I want you to remember that God gives us faith that can outlast His silence. God places no limitations on faith, and faith places no limitations on God. Wherever you are now is just temporary. Don't allow the temporary to frustrate the eternal promise God has given you. If He has called you to higher ground, you cannot stay where you are forever. A time is soon coming for you to arrive in high places.

First Samuel 14 tells a story about Jonathan, the son of Saul. At that time, the Israelite army was hiding in the caves of Gibeah from the Philistines. Without seeking the Lord's advice, Saul foolishly had declared war over this enemy. But Saul's Israelites were outnumbered and under armed. Saul and his son Jonathan had the only weapons, one sword each. Their soldiers had only farm tools for weapons (see 1 Samuel 13).

Despite the weight of discouragement that fell over Saul and his army, Jonathan stepped up. He told his armorbearer, "Come, let us go over to the Philistines' garrison that is on the other side" (1 Samuel 14:1). Jonathan believed God was going to do something and deliver the enemy into their hands. As Jonathan climbed toward the enemy's garrison, he found himself stuck between one sharp rock and another; we might say he was literally stuck between a rock and a hard place.

If you're in between a rock and a hard place right now, rejoice. You're in the right place. The only thing that's left is for God to help you get over to the other side!

Saul was nearby when Jonathan made his decision to go. Unaware of his son's bravery, Saul was sitting under a pomegranate tree, chomping on some fruit, and saying "It's too hard!" Jonathan, on the other hand, took a faith-filled initiative and said, in effect, "I refuse to let any hard place stop me from reaching my high place."

The spirit of retreat had settled over Saul, just as it has settled over many people today. He sat in the shade, waiting for better timing, an easier strategy or more help. But God knows that high places are only reached through hard places. If we want to live out what God has promised us, sometimes we're going to need to get up and go get it. Seeking the hard places may sound counterintuitive, but like Jonathan, we must decide to go seek them.

You cannot have a miracle without a crisis. It is the crisis that produces the miracle. If you are going through the biggest crisis you've ever been through in your life, it means you are nearer to the greatest miracle you've ever experienced!

The Israelites were in a crisis. But to get to the miracle they needed, they had to go over the hard place. Jonathan's plan was that he and his armorbearer would show themselves to the Philistines, and if the enemy said, "We're going to come to you," they would stay right where they were. If they said, "Come up to us," the two men would go up and it would be a sign that the Lord would deliver the Philistines into their hands (see 1 Samuel 14:8–11).

When these two men appeared before the Philistines, the enemy soldiers said, "Come up to us, and we will show you something" (verse 12). So Jonathan and his armorbearer started climbing and got into such a narrow place that they had to crawl on their hands and knees to get through. Yet that day, through a supernatural miracle, the Lord saved Israel and defeated the Philistines. What a picture! When we use our hands and knees in prayer and praise, we are not going to die in that in-between place. We are closer to higher ground than ever before!

I want to remind you of someone else who was also between a rock and a hard place. After Jesus was crucified and was pronounced dead, Roman soldiers took His body and put it in the hewn-out rock of a borrowed tomb. They laid His body atop this slab of rock and then rolled a huge stone in front of the tomb to seal it shut. In their minds, Jesus was never getting out. But when it was the right time, when Jesus had waited long enough, He stepped out—alive. And He is whispering to you today, *Because I made it through My rock and My hard place, you are going to make it through yours.*

I don't know how painful or scary or discouraging your hard place is today, but I'm here to tell you that you are headed for higher ground.

Dig Out of Depression

When you are overwhelmed by a spirit of depression, you feel empty. You can barely get out of bed. You force yourself to do the simplest things. It's not the passing feeling of a bad day or a case of the blues; it's a heavy weight of despair.

It's a feeling King David knew all too well. In fact, this man wrote much of the book of Psalms, a work of beautiful poetry that reflects language that is not always optimistic, but is real and raw. If he felt alone, he said so. If he felt downcast, he wrote about it. If he felt depressed, David was not ashamed to make it known.

Weak, but Still Anointed

After David was anointed king by the prophet Samuel, he found himself on the run from King Saul, who was trying to kill him. After Saul's death, the nation of Israel divided into two kingdoms. King David ruled the southern portion, consisting only of the tribe of Judah. King Ishbosheth, one of Saul's sons, reigned over Israel, which included the remaining tribes.

One day, King Ishbosheth got into a fight with his military leader, Abner (see 2 Samuel 3). Abner had secretly approached King David and proposed that Israel should be united as one nation. Knowing that God had anointed David to be king over all Israel, Abner defected to David's rule and pledged loyalty to him. This was the moment David had dreamed about. *This is what I've been believing. This is why I've been anointed. This is the reason for all I've gone through these many years, running and hiding in exile, and living in caves like some kind of animal. Now, this is my big moment!*

But there was one problem. Right before the deal was sealed to unite both kingdoms and put David on the throne to rule over it all, the whole thing blew up. Joab, David's chief military commander, held a grudge against Abner because Abner had accidentally killed Joab's brother. When Joab saw Abner hanging around David, he began to seethe. And then, wanting revenge, Joab slaughtered Abner. In that moment, everything David had been waiting for fell to pieces. Yet this was when David made one of the most profound statements of his life. In response to the murder of Abner, David said, "I am weak today, though anointed king" (2 Samuel 3:39).

What a contrast—to see that David had so much power, yet experienced weakness at the same time. Did you know that it's possible to be weak and still be anointed? The Bible says in 1 Peter 2:9 that those of us who have put our faith in Jesus Christ are a royal priesthood. Revelation 1:6 mentions that God has raised us to be kings and priests in His Kingdom. When you think of royalty, what comes to mind? Strength? Power? Confidence?

Did you know that it's possible to be anointed and weak? Here's a secret: You will experience seasons where you feel weak, but it does not change the authority you have in every situation. Weakness and divine anointing stand together.

Sometimes, when we're groaning, *I am weak, I am depressed, I can't do this,* God's greatest purpose is on its way into our life. God intends His greatest marvels to come when we're at our lowest. You can be weak on particular days, but know that God does not give up on you.

The Kingdom of God is one of opposites. It's possible to be poor yet rich, to have joy in the midst of sorrow, peace in the middle of a storm. Paul wrote that he took pleasure in his weaknesses: "Therefore I take pleasure in infirmities, in reproaches, in needs, in persecutions, in distresses, for Christ's sake. For when I am weak, then I am strong" (2 Corinthians 12:10). On the surface, that certainly makes no sense!

I can't tell you how many times I've wondered why the children of God can feel depressed. And not only can we wrestle with that weighty emotion, but we can also struggle with oppressive clinical depression. I know many Christians who feel massive guilt because of it. Even if you love and serve God, you might be burdened by depression because your marriage is on the verge of collapse, your child is on his or her sixth rehab program, or you just can't seem to snap out of what your doctor called postpartum depression, even though your baby just turned six.

Depression attempts to steal your identity from you. But depression is not who you are. You must define yourself not by your circumstance, but by your identity. You may be weak on the outside, but on the inside you are anointed. You may be depressed, but your truest identity is that you are part of a royal priesthood.

> You may be weak on the outside, but on the inside you are anointed. You may be depressed, but your truest identity is that you are part of a royal priesthood.

You know who was the first person to attempt identity theft? The devil! Isaiah 14:13 records him saying, "I will ascend into heaven, I will exalt my throne above the stars of God; I will also sit on the mount of the congregation on the farthest sides of the north." He wanted to steal God's identity and be like God. The enemy desires to do the same thing to you—steal your God-given identity.

Now, the devil doesn't want to steal your identity to be you. He just doesn't want you to use your identity as an anointed king or queen. He doesn't want you to believe that you are anointed. He doesn't want you trusting that even if depression has a hold on you, you are still a child of God. That's how powerful he knows your identity in God is! If he can get you to abandon who you believe you are, he wins!

Just because you have suffered loss, just because you're in a bind and have no answers, just because your flesh is weak and you've lost your joy, you must never forget that you are still an anointed king or queen in the Kingdom of God.

Make this confession right now: "I may be weak, but I'm still anointed."

Hope in the Wayside

Mark 10:46–52 tells the story of a blind man named Bartimaeus who was begging on the side of the road. Instead of saying "the side of the road," some translations use the term *wayside*. Bartimaeus was living a life without motion, stranded on the wayside of life. He wasn't going anywhere. He lacked purpose. He was just sitting on the side of the road as life passed him by, hoping someone would throw him a few crumbs out of pity.

Ever feel as if you're sitting on the wayside? So bogged down by depression, the cares of this world, the responsibilities of caring for others, the pressure of trying to live your best life, that you just go numb? And you resign yourself to sitting on the sidelines of your life. No joy. No intention. Just getting by and taking what you can. Bartimaeus may have been on the wayside, but Jesus noticed him, and He notices you, too. He notices people who are stuck in that place.

Jesus told a parable about a sower who scattered seeds in many places (see Matthew 13). Some seeds fell on stony ground, some fell among thorns, some fell on good ground, and others fell *by the wayside* (see verse 4). I'm glad that when the sower sowed seed, some of it fell by the wayside. That's where it might reach someone like Bartimaeus. Or you. Or me. Most of us have spent some time in the ditches of life, and when somebody's life is off track like that, the only thing that can get him or her out of the ditch is the seed of God's Word. The birds may have snatched up the seed in the parable Jesus told, but this image still reminds us of the potential present on the wayside of life. Even there, God can scatter the seed of His Word to us.

Beggars in the time of Bartimaeus wore a sort of uniform. According to historians and scholars, it was a garment issued by the Roman government that confirmed the wearers as official beggars who were allowed to be where they were, asking people for money. Think of their outfit as a license to beg. Beggars had that right. They had the right to situate themselves by the wayside and engage with others only to accept their help or pity.

Have you ever thought you had a right to be angry? Or bitter? Or depressed? In this sense, I'm not talking about clinical depression that stems from severe chemical imbalances. I'm talking about when something unjust, traumatic or painful happens and you therefore feel you have a license to be depressed and refuse to engage in life. I don't want to minimize anyone's traumatic past or say it wasn't that bad. But I want to tell you that you will not overcome that state of being until you forfeit your right to be on the wayside.

What happens when we cling to our right to be depressed? A root of bitterness begins to grow in our hearts. When Jesus comes along, He messes with our pity party. Even though Bartimaeus had a right to be where he was, had the necessary beggar's garment, Scripture says that he had heard about Jesus (see Mark 10:47). Faith always begins at the point of hearing. When this blind man heard it was

Jesus passing by, he cried, "Jesus, Son of David, have mercy on me!" Many people warned him to be quiet, but he cried out all the more, "Son of David, have mercy on me!" (Mark 10:47–48).

When Bartimaeus cried out to Jesus the first time, those around him told him to hold his peace. The enemy wants us to do the same. Shut our mouth. Zip it. Don't praise. Don't speak of someplace better than where we are right now. Don't talk victory. If the enemy can get you and me to stay quiet, he can keep us in our place.

A powerful way to get out of the place you are in is when you begin to open your mouth and speak about Jesus. The last thing the devil wants you to do is to open your mouth and start speaking the promises of God and praise to the Lord. But that's the first thing we must do in order to overcome.

We need to send our words out in the direction we want them to go. In other words, we need to start talking victory when we're staring at defeat. We need to start talking healing when we're feeling sick. We need to start talking blessing when we don't have anything. We need to talk about marching when we feel like quitting.

Proverbs 15:4 tells us, "A wholesome tongue is a tree of life." What comes out of your mouth after you open it matters. Your tongue can turn the worst situation in your life, the situation that's causing bitterness to well up and poison your spirit, into a situation that brings God the glory.

Open your mouth and start to sing. Pray. Read the Bible aloud. Memorize and recite Scripture as you would personal affirmations. Take Paul's recommendation and call the things that are not as though they are (see Romans 4:17). This is faith.

I know I talked in the previous chapter about faith being a tool to overcome discouragement. Faith is one of the greatest tools to overcome anything! But it's more than just believing in your heart. Faith's power is activated through your senses, through hearing and confessing.

Jesus stood still amidst the commotion around that day and sent for Bartimaeus. "And throwing aside his garment, he rose and came to Jesus" (Mark 10:50). You see what happened there? Bartimaeus tore off his beggar's garment and then got up and walked to Jesus. He couldn't see Jesus yet. He hadn't been healed. He hadn't even been given a promise that he would regain his sight. Even though the man who was blind didn't see anything concerning a miracle, he heard the voice of Jesus and started moving at the command of the voice. He was acting as though he were healed before his healing happened! And before Bartimaeus stood up to walk toward Jesus, he threw off his beggar's garment. He dumped his right to be depressed, dysfunctional and deadlocked.

I don't know what's happened to you, but I know what the enemy whispers to us to keep us by the wayside: *Anyone who has been through your pain has a right to have a few drinks. Anyone who feels so alone in a marriage has a right to spend and spend and spend and rack up debt. You lost your mom when you were young . . . your dad was a deadbeat . . . so of course you're addicted—and you have every right to stay there.*

But I know there's a deeper desperation for freedom inside you than the pain of being wronged, hurt or robbed. Inside you is a man or woman who is desperate to overcome.

Like Bartimaeus, you may be sitting on life's wayside, waiting there because you think that's what you deserve. I'm here to tell you there's a better way. God is here to breathe new life into your spirit. Your future depends on it!

Get Rid of the *ANTS*

So how do we get out of the wayside ditch? Sometimes the only way to get back to God's path of life is to get our thinking right. One day in the early 1990s, psychiatrist Dr. Daniel Amen had a hard day at the office. He met with several patients, including four people who were suicidal, two teen runaways and two married couples who couldn't stand each other. He came home that evening to a kitchen infested with ants. As he was cleaning up the critters, he imagined these insects' name as an acronym for *Automatic Negative Thoughts* (*ANT*). He realized that, just as his kitchen was infested with ants, his patients' brains were infested with automatic negative thoughts that destroyed their well-being.[1]

I like to use Dr. Amen's acronym this way: *Automatic Negative Thinking Syndrome*, or *ANTS*. When you automatically think about the worst-case scenario right off the bat, you're suffering from an infestation of *ANTS*. This syndrome fuels negativity and incites depression. Instead of thinking positive thoughts or hoping for the best, we instantly think that the worst is going to happen. If a potential job opportunity comes our way, we assume we're not qualified.

When the Israelites were freed from Egyptian slavery and were on their way to the Promised Land, they had *ANTS* on the brain: *There's no way we're getting through the Red Sea. We're not going to have enough to eat or drink. We've been at this forever; we're never going to get there. The giants in the land are too big; they'll never let us into the land.*

What they didn't think was: *God brought us through Egypt; surely He can get us through a sea. It's time for God to show off in another miracle. God did it once; He can do it again. He set us free before; now He is going to do greater things.*

The Israelites' thoughts automatically turned negative once they hit an obstacle. And I know the feeling. Back when I began my work as a pastor at Free Chapel, I was a bit insecure. I was familiar with the life of a traveling evangelist because I had done that for years. But pastoring was a whole new thing. At the time, I was starting to get to know our board of directors, and they were getting to know me.

A few months in, after an amazing church service, I walked through the hallway to get to my office. I noticed four or five of the board members huddled up, whispering. As soon as they saw me, they broke it up really quickly. My ears burned, and I felt *ANTS* crawling up the side of my face. Immediately, the negativity took over my brain: *They don't like you. They're talking about you. They're not happy with all the changes you're making in the church.* For the next week, *ANTS* was all I could think about. I cried. I prayed. I even told Cherise we ought to be prepared to get fired. I was ready for the worst.

The following Sunday, the same men who I was convinced were going to fire me pulled me aside into a little room. I took a deep breath, preparing myself for a speech that would begin something like, "Before we start, let me just tell you something. . . ."

One of the board members piped up before I had the chance: "Pastor, we love you and Cherise. We love your family. We're having such a move of God in this church, and we wanted to do something for you and your growing family. We noticed that you need a van, and we have decided as a church to provide you with one."

The man smiled as he gently pressed a set of car keys into the palm of my hand.

I was so ashamed, I almost didn't receive it!

Don't let *ANTS* infest your mind. We serve a powerful God. We serve a faithful God. He is not out to decimate, devour and destroy you. He is a good God. He is on your side. He is for you.

If you have an *ANTS* infestation, "be transformed by the renewing of your mind" (Romans 12:2). Renew your mind with what God says in His Word. Read the Bible. Meditate on it. Memorize it. Soak in its truth. You'll get rid of the Automatic Negative Thoughts Syndrome that way and start living with the right information instead.

Think Yourself Happy

Paul gave us a great example in the Scriptures of choosing to set his mind on what was right. We read in the book of Acts how

Paul endured shipwrecks, beatings, arrest and even prison multiple times. In Acts 26, we find him standing before King Agrippa to testify on behalf of himself, in defense of his very life. The king looks at Paul and says, "All right, Paul, do you have anything to say?" I love Paul's response: "I think myself happy, King Agrippa" (verse 2).

I am not saying that you can simply think all of your problems away, or that no one ever needs outside help or counsel. But when it comes to your day-to-day attitude and the way you face the world when you get up in the morning, do you know how you get happy? You *think* yourself happy! You know how you get depressed? You *think* yourself depressed. Paul was clear. His circumstances did not dictate his happiness; no, he *thought* himself happy.

Here's a secret if you haven't learned it yet: A narrow mind is always accompanied by a big mouth. And negative words bring on negative feelings. When things turn sour, our first inclination is to get depressed. The feeling may be a natural one, but it doesn't have to be a permanent one. Think yourself happy.

You have a choice. You always do. You can focus on the problem, or you can choose to focus on the promises of God.

Keep in mind that this is not mind over matter. It's not merely a state of positivity. It's a decision. It's a choice to live by faith and not by fear. With Paul, we're talking about a guy who was minutes away from being executed, and yet through the power of God, he decided to think himself happy. Daniel was happy in the lions' den. Shadrach, Meshach and Abed-Nego were dancing in the fire.

All of us are born into certain conditions. We don't have any say about those conditions, but we have a lot to say about the choices that we make in life. You have a choice. You always do. You can focus on the problem, or you can choose to focus on the promises of God.

More than Halfway

You may be pummeled by the aftershocks of a personal tragedy and be thinking, *Pastor Jentezen, trying to get rid of ANTS, meditating on the Bible and spending time in worship are great and all, but I am so devastated in my spirit that my future seems hopeless. I barely have the strength and the motivation to get through the rest of my day.*

I want to tell you a story about a man named Terah. He was Abraham's father, and he is first introduced to us in the Bible in the genealogy portion of Genesis 11. Within this ancestral information, there's a reference to a personal tragedy: "Now Terah lived seventy years, and begot Abram, Nahor, and Haran. This is the genealogy of Terah: Terah begot Abram, Nahor, and Haran. Haran begot Lot. And Haran died before his father Terah in his native land, in Ur of the Chaldeans" (Genesis 11:26–28).

We might assume from this text that Haran died chronologically before Terah, but what the Scripture actually means is that Haran died in the presence of, or in front of, his father. So Terah watched his son die. To anyone, especially any parent, this is incomprehensible. Some of you have felt that kind of pain, and for that, I am so sorry.

The Bible tells us this about Terah:

> And Terah took his son Abram and his grandson Lot, the son of Haran, and his daughter-in-law Sarai, his son Abram's wife, and they went out with them from Ur of the Chaldeans to go to the land of Canaan; and they came to Haran and dwelt there. So the days of Terah were two hundred and five years, and Terah died in Haran.
>
> Genesis 11:31–32

Terah and his family were on a journey to Canaan. It was God's destiny for them to enter the Promised Land. But something strange happened on the way there. As Terah began to work through and heal over his son's death, pressing into the future and holding tight to what God had promised him, he came to a city called Haran. And Terah died there, in a city with the same name as his lost son.

I believe what happened is that Terah reentered the place of his grief. I believe that sorrow overtook him. As his heart began to cry out for his son, he stayed there in Haran. And never left. Because Terah settled in Haran, he never made it to Canaan. He died in the city that bore the same name of his deceased son, and that represented his reentry into grief.

I don't expect anyone who has lost a loved one just to get over it. That would be foolish and ignorant. But I've seen how people process grief differently. Some hold fast to it for the rest of their lives. Others—only through the grace of God—find a way to heal from the tragedy in a way that doesn't deny the pain, but that allows them to access God's destiny for their lives.

Have you ever let a past wound nullify what God has in store for you? Have you ever settled in a place that wasn't bad, but wasn't God's best for you either, because of an open wound you never allowed to heal?

No matter how painful a situation we have gone through, God has a place of purpose and a destiny for our lives. We may enter it limping. We may cry our way there. We may nurse a broken heart while reaching for the plans God laid out for us even before we were put on this earth. And that's okay.

God's will for our lives is not to settle for halfway. He hasn't planned for us to enjoy a little bit of happiness, or live expecting the next shoe to drop, or live nursing a wound and giving little thought to healing. You may have lost someone special, but God is not through with your life. Don't allow your future to be held hostage at Haran. God has a Canaan for each of us!

One of my favorite verses of Scripture is Jeremiah 15:16: "Your words were found, and I ate them, and Your word was to me the joy and rejoicing of my heart; for I am called by Your name, O Lord God of hosts." Now, I don't think that the prophet Jeremiah, the author of these words, was literally eating the Word of God for a snack. But Jeremiah was offering us a powerful analogy: Just as food brings strength to the body, the Word of God brings nourishment and energy to a hurting soul. The Word of God is sustenance for a broken spirit.

When my dad died suddenly at the age of 56 from a massive heart attack, my mom was devastated. In her greatest time of sorrow and grief, she held onto this Scripture:

> Though the fig tree may not blossom, nor fruit be on the vines; though the labor of the olive may fail, and the fields yield no food; though the flock may be cut off from the fold, and there be no herd in the stalls— yet I will rejoice in the Lord, I will joy in the God of my salvation.
>
> The Lord God is my strength; He will make my feet like deer's feet, and He will make me walk on my high hills.
>
> Habakkuk 3:17–19

Mom could relate well to the beginning of this passage. She felt alone, devastated, in a place of brokenness, empty, her whole life thrown into a whirlwind. But as she clung to this passage of Scripture day after day, sometimes minute after minute, she felt God speaking to her heart: *Even though the ground isn't giving forth fruit, and even though you're not seeing the things that I promised you would see, don't stop rejoicing in Me. You will walk in high places.*

Although her grief seemed endless, by faith she moved from North Carolina to Gainesville, Georgia. There, she became a pastor on staff at our church, Free Chapel. She started a gathering for seniors called the Wisdom Club, which would turn into our seniors' ministry and wind up having hundreds of seniors a month get together and fellowship. She also started services at rest homes.

173

The demand for these grew so fast that she began to form teams to accommodate the requests, and the ministry held about 38 services a month. Mom also started a ministry that delivered food to grieving families. Today, at 85 years old, she still serves on staff at Free Chapel.

There's no telling the number of people Mom has reached through her outpouring of service. What if Mom had settled in the place of her grief? What if she had not moved on and allowed God to use her dreams to expand His Kingdom?

Refuse to get stuck in a permanent place of grief. It's not over, even if it looks as though it is. God had a Canaan beyond my mom's Haran, and He has a promised land for you, too.

Become a Prisoner of Hope

What happens in the hardest times of our lives is that we become prisoners of the feelings that overwhelm us—feelings like fear, discouragement and depression. But God is offering us a different way of living. He is calling us "prisoners of hope." I love the wording in Zechariah 9:12: "Return to the stronghold, you prisoners of hope. Even today I declare that I will restore double to you."

The way I see it, you're either going to be chained to your pain or to your hope. If you have suffered loss, are in pain or lack purpose, don't worry. It takes one step, a little nudge, a slight turn and a bit of hope to turn the tide. Instead of being imprisoned by what will hold you back, become a prisoner of what will set you free.

Depression is a real and serious condition. I urge you to seek the advice of your doctor, a licensed therapist or counselor, or a pastor if you feel you are depressed and unable to function. I'd also like to share with you four helpful tips licensed counselor Shana Ruff provided me with that will help you find your way back home from the clutch of depression:

Reach out

- You have to *reach out* for help when you are going through things. There is restoration on the other side of your reach. (See the story of the man with the withered hand in Matthew 12.)
- Be careful to reach out to the right person. Make sure he or she is a trusted individual, someone to whom you can take your "withered hand" or vulnerabilities.
- See Proverbs 11:14.

Speak out

- After you reach out to a trusted person, then you *speak out*. You have to tell that person what's going on (see Psalm 32:3–5).
- When you keep silent, it eats you up on the inside. Only when you bring what's hidden into the light do you get healed.
- God can't heal what you conceal!
- See James 5:16.

Get out

- After you have reached out and spoken out, you begin to walk out the journey of healing and *get out*. This process may take some time, or it could happen instantly.
- See Luke 8:28, 35.
- What encounters are you having with Jesus? Praise, worship, prayer, fasting, etc.?

Help out

- After you reach out, speak out and get out, then it's your turn to *help out*!
- Take the opportunity to use your story to help someone else.
- When God has healed you, set you free and delivered you, you need to tell it!
- Help someone who may be struggling in the same area that you struggled in.
- See 2 Corinthians 1:3–4.

Fight the Flesh

It's not difficult to see how the enemy uses our own flesh to destroy our relationships and our families. Sexual sin without repentance will cause you to lose your mission, your common sense and God's anointing. We can be overcome or defeated by the desires of the flesh, depending on what we choose to say, listen to and look at.

Every second of every day, 28,258 people are watching pornography. One in five mobile searches is for pornography. Every second on the internet, $3,075.64 is spent on porn.[1] Globally, porn is an estimated $97 billion industry. And $12 billion of that comes from the United States.[2] A study that investigated porn consumption in different countries connected increased acts of sexual aggression with pornography use in both males and females.[3]

Is pornography a problem? According to Barna Group research, today's young people don't think so. Teens and young adults rank not recycling as more immoral than viewing porn.[4]

If you think pornography's millions of viewers are people outside the Church, think again. The following stats illuminate how pervasive pornography is inside Christian culture:

- 64 percent of Christian men and 15 percent of Christian women say they watch porn at least once a month.
- 1 in 5 youth pastors and 1 in 7 senior pastors use porn on a regular basis and acknowledge a struggle with porn.
- 43 percent of senior pastors and youth pastors say they have struggled with pornography in the past.[5]

We've moved from dirty magazines to searching for anything we want with the click of a button, and now we're gearing up for virtual reality porn, expected to be a $1 billion business by 2025. Porn makes a ton of money, but at what cost? When it comes to divorce, 56 percent involve one party having "an obsessive interest in pornographic websites."[6] Rather than fostering connection, porn perpetuates social isolation and begets loneliness.

But watching or being involved in pornography isn't the only path to sexual immorality. According to the American Association for Marriage and Family Therapy, national surveys indicate that 15 percent of married women and 25 percent of married men have had extramarital affairs. The incidence is about 20 percent higher when emotional and sexual relationships without intercourse are included.[7] Over half of Christians say sex before marriage in a committed relationship is sometimes or always okay.[8]

We have fallen so far off the mark. Unless you make up your mind to honor God with your body and maintain sexual integrity, you will be at the mercy of the lust of your flesh.

God still has standards.

God still has a moral code.

God still has barriers we ought to honor that will help preserve our character, our reputation, our name, our family, our marriage, our anointing.

Enter Jezebel

As we talked about in chapter 8, the spirit of Jezebel continues to make appearances in various ways even long after that wicked queen's death. We saw one instance recorded in Matthew 14, but let's take a brief second look as a reminder of what this evil spirit is like. Remember how John the Baptist had given King Herod a message that he didn't want to hear, so John ended up in prison as a result? Herod's wife, Herodias, had become angry and bitter because John had humiliated her openly by telling her husband, "It's not right for you to marry your brother's wife, and you are living in adultery."

Then, on the night of Herod's birthday feast, when Herodias brought her own daughter out to perform in front of the king and his guests, it was quickly obvious that this wasn't a modest performance like reciting a poem or playing the piano in a frock. The daughter was scantily clad, and whatever she did in her provocative dance, it so entranced King Herod that in his drunken stupor he said, "You have pleased me so much with this that I'll give you anything you ask, up to half the kingdom." At the nudging of her mother, the girl gave her answer: "Give me John the Baptist's head here on a platter" (Matthew 14:8).

This was the manipulative spirit of Jezebel at work, using lust to fulfill the works of the enemy. The same enemy hunts us down today, tempting us through what we scroll through on our phones, what we see as we walk by something, how we feel when someone brushes up against us. This spirit preys on our loneliness or insecurity to get us to search for satisfaction in places we know we shouldn't.

The dance on the screen may mesmerize you, but in the end it will demand your head on a platter. Reject the spirit of Jezebel. In the rest of this chapter, I will offer you practical advice on how to reject Jezebel and choose sexual integrity.

Trade Your Shame for Honor

Before we get to that advice, however, I want to talk about the shame that you may already be experiencing as you read this. Let's trade that shame for honor, a purposefulness that will inspire integrity instead. Sexual sin has a way of loading people with guilt and shame to the point that they are afraid to come clean with God. Listen to me: God does not define you by your worst mistake. He does not look at you as though you are your addiction. You may be involved in things you are ashamed of, but forgiveness through Jesus is readily available to you. When you ask God to forgive you, He will not remind you of what you've done. He will not replay how hard you've fallen off track.

The enemy, however, will try to convince you that your sin has derailed the will of God for your life. That is a lie from the pit of hell. God is greater than sin. His grace is greater than sin. God has not changed His mind about you. His call on your life is irrevocable. It doesn't matter if you've struggled with pornography for years, lived with your boyfriend or just ended an extramarital affair. If you repent and ask God for forgiveness, He will wipe your slate clean and will not shame you for what you have done.

Your purpose is stronger than your sin. God wants you to burst into a new beginning. In Isaiah 61:7 God promises, "Instead of your shame you shall have double honor."

When Jesus hung on the cross, the Bible says He not only bore our griefs, but He carried our shame (see Isaiah 53:4). He carried the humiliation, the embarrassment, the mess-ups, the failure. Every one of us was born with a shame nature. We inherited it from Adam and Eve. When they sinned, they hid. And they hid because they were ashamed.

Although God knew what Adam and Eve had done and He sees what we do, His love never changes. His willingness to forgive does not falter. Instead of shame, He gives us a double portion of honor.

Not because we finally got our life back together. Not because we stopped sinning. And not because we earned it somehow through piling on the good works. No, we receive honor for our shame because God loves us so much that He sent His Son to die on a cross, and to rise again after death, to set us free from sin and shame.

You don't have to beat yourself up; God doesn't. If this is hitting home, it's time to break the chains of shame. Now is the time to choose sexual integrity and to live in honor of who God has made you to be.

It's time to get up, get out and get free.

It's time to get up, get out and get free.

Before you continue reading, if you're feeling the heaviness of shame weighing on your heart, I'd like you to read aloud the following prayer—or say a prayer in your own words. Don't allow your past sins or addictions to keep you from living the life God has designed for you.

> *Dear God, I have been struggling with guilt and shame from some of the past mistakes I have made. Today, I ask You to help me walk with integrity. Give me a brand-new start. I surrender my entire life to You.*
>
> *Today, I am committing never to turn back. I receive Your forgiveness, and I ask You to replace my shame with a double portion of honor. By Your power, I am going to live a pure life for Your glory. I know my story isn't over. Thank You for loving me and giving me a life filled with purpose and hope. Amen.*

Your story isn't over. It's time for you to write the next chapter of it.

Keep Your Underwear On

After miraculously delivering the Israelites from the bondage of slavery in Egypt, God wanted His people to be free to worship Him, to live and to prosper. As they began to walk with Him, He established specific rules for their worship, sacrifice, holiness and even their attire. Approaching God's holy presence in those days required a certain level of purity.

God's presence was manifest in the Ark of the Covenant, which was housed in the Temple, or earlier in the special tents designed to represent the Temple. You couldn't just walk into God's presence back then with sin in your life. God made it clear to Moses that the priests would die if they entered the Holy Place with sin in their lives, or if they were unclean or impure in their presentation. To protect them, God described how the priests of the Old Testament were to approach the Most Holy Place, where the Ark was housed. Detailed instructions were given for the making of their robes, ephods and other clothing items.

By their outward appearance, it was clear to anybody they passed on the street that Aaron and his sons were priests. But anyone can put on an outer garment and look the part. How many people do you know who look like Christians but who live entirely different lifestyles? God always sees deeper than the surface. Some of God's provisions are surprisingly simple, as simple as keeping your under-wear on. In Exodus 28:42–43, after specifying the composition of the priests' outer appearance, God said to Moses,

> Make linen undergarments as a covering for the body, reaching from the waist to the thigh. Aaron and his sons must wear them whenever they enter the tent of meeting or approach the altar to minister in the Holy Place, so that they will not incur guilt and die.

That's how the New International Version reads. But the New King James says it this way:

> And you shall make for them linen trousers to cover their nakedness; they shall reach from the waist to the thighs. They shall be on Aaron

and on his sons when they come into the tabernacle of meeting, or when they come near the altar to minister in the holy place, that they do not incur iniquity and die.

Let's look at a word you may have overlooked in these passages: *incur*, which the dictionary defines as "to come into or acquire (some consequence, usually undesirable or injurious) . . . to become liable or subject to through one's own action; bring or take upon oneself."[9]

Seems like there is a simple, God-given solution for not incurring iniquity and dying: Keep your underwear on! And because God declared at the end of verse 43, "It shall be a statute forever to him and his descendants after him," this advice still holds true for us today. In other words, no matter what the prevailing norms of the day say, God's simple advice from Exodus will still help you.

If you think this is just about a dress code, you will miss the deeper truth God is trying to communicate. This is about a more complete idea of purity. It's not just living a good life and being a good person by the world's standards. It's not enough just to go to church, where people look at your outward appearance and say, "Man, this person really has a walk with God." People may see what's on the outside, but just as with Aaron's sons, God knows what's going on in your private life. The only ones who knew whether or not Aaron's sons had their underwear on were Aaron's sons and God. Everybody else thought that they looked holy. Whether they were or were not was in full view of the God who sees all. He knew then, and thousands of years later, He still knows.

If God sacrificed one of His own creations to provide clothing for naked Adam and Eve, who do you think is always trying to rip off everybody's clothes? Think about it. Remember Joseph's story of becoming a slave and then a ruler? He was a handsome, talented young guy, but talent will take you to places where only character can keep you.

The story of Joseph is a classic example of clothing yourself in every kind of purity. Joseph found himself supervising the entire household of an Egyptian official named Potiphar, the captain of the guard. His master's beautiful wife took notice of Joseph and urged, "Come to bed with me!" But he refused.

That doesn't mean it wasn't a difficult decision, but it was the right decision. Joseph told her, "How then can I do this great wickedness, and sin against God?" (Genesis 39:9). Though she spoke to Joseph day after day, he refused to go to bed with her.

That's what it looks like to be pure of heart. Joseph's talents and abilities put him in a position of trust and authority, but only an excellent character could keep him from abusing his master's trust.

If you think being pure or making the right decisions makes you immune to criticism or even false accusation, think again. Not everyone will get goose bumps because of your commitment to God and to doing right. Misery loves company, and so does sin. Refusing to "go along to get along" can oftentimes bring criticism and a shrinking friendship network. Do the right thing anyway.

Potiphar's wife would not take no for an answer. One day Joseph went into the house to attend to his duties, and none of the household servants were inside. She caught him by his coat and invited him to bed yet again. He fled, leaving his coat in her hand as he ran out of the house. Sometimes you need to do more than just say no; you need to flee. She may have gotten his coat, but she didn't get his character. Joseph kept his underwear on.

Do you know where the word *fornication* comes from, or what it means? It refers to any sexual relationships outside the bonds of marriage. Seven lists of sins can be found in the letters of the apostle Paul, and fornication is first on five of those lists (see 1 Corinthians 5:11; Colossians 3:5). The root of that word is *fornex*, which referred to a specific part of an ancient coliseum. At the coliseum in Ephesus, for example, thousands of people would gather to be entertained by the sight of Christians being tortured and then martyred for their faith. Unclothed prostitutes would wait in the foyer of the coliseum, calling out to those leaving to have sex with them, while the blood of Christians still soaked into the ground. That scene is where we get today's word *fornication*, having to do with sexual activity of any kind outside marriage.

Did you ever consider that your Bible teaches that nudity outside the bonds of holy matrimony is associated with demonic powers? Read Mark 5:1–20, the story of the demoniac who fell at the feet of Jesus in Gadara. The man had about two thousand demons tormenting him night and day, and the primary manifestation of that torment was that he would strip off all his clothes and run naked through the tombs, screaming and cutting himself with rocks.

When Jesus set this person free and cast the demons out of him, the town was astonished to see the man "clothed and in his right mind" (verse 15). I believe there is a connection in Scripture between demonic power and the unclothing of both America and other cultures around the world. Proverbs 6:27 says, "Can a man take fire to his bosom, and his clothes not be burned?"

If you are sitting around a campfire and you decide to take a shovelful of hot, burning coals and dump them in your lap, what would happen? The first and most obvious thing is that your clothes would be burned off, swiftly followed by a few layers of skin! The writer of Proverbs used that extreme example to make a critical point: The fire of lust can burn off your clothes—and your purity—if you let it.

Keeping our clothes on depends on the decisions we make about what we allow into our lives. What you listen to, what you look at and what you meditate on all affect your ability to make the decisions necessary to live a holy life. I have had young people (and adults) come to me and say, "I just can't live holy. I have such a hard time. I can't stop sleeping around." Do you know why you can't stop? You can't stop because you keep taking in the "fire" that burns your clothes off. What you put into your life contributes to—or chips away at—your sexual purity. I cannot even write in these pages the words to so many popular songs today because the lyrics are foul. I have spoken at conferences where thousands of teens rededicate their lives to Christ, only to leave with their headphones on and their earbuds in, listening to the same music they listened to before they made their decision. If you call yourself a Christian and you are constantly burning lyrics and images like that into your mind, you might as well just dump those hot coals right into your lap. You would have just as much of a chance at keeping your clothes on.

The enemy likes to use a bow-and-arrow approach. He stands at a distance, shooting fiery darts into your mind, to watch and see how you will respond. That's why Paul warned us to clothe ourselves with the whole armor of God, holding up the shield of faith to fight off those fiery darts (see Ephesians 6:10–20). Don't entertain "hot" thoughts. Clothe yourself in the righteousness of God. And clothe yourself in the literal clothes God has given you. Pursue the purity of heart that fills you, until there is no room for the spirit of lust or the illicit desires of the flesh.

Beware the Traveler

In the Old Testament, the prophet Nathan called King David out for having an adulterous affair with a woman named Bathsheba. It started one day when David was at home in the palace. From the palace's rooftop, David saw a beautiful woman bathing (see 2 Samuel 11). Smitten by Bathsheba, he asked around about her and found out she was married. That didn't seem to bother David since he sent for her and slept with her anyway. She ended up getting pregnant. In the hope of concealing the true identity of the baby's father, David tried to trick Bathsheba's husband into returning from battle so he would go home and sleep with his wife. Then, when her husband would not go home since the men he fought alongside could not do likewise, David sent him back to the battlefield, onto the front lines, where he was killed.

The prophet Nathan comes along and confronts David by telling him a story:

> There were two men in one city, one rich and the other poor. The rich man had exceedingly many flocks and herds. But the poor man had nothing, except one little ewe lamb which he had bought and nourished; and it grew up together with him and with his children. It ate of his own food and drank from his own cup and lay in his bosom; and it was like a daughter to him. And a traveler came to the rich man, who refused to take from his own flock and from his own herd to prepare one for the wayfaring man who had come to him; but he took the poor man's lamb and prepared it for the man who had come to him.
>
> 2 Samuel 12:1–4

David, of course, is the rich man who stole the "lamb," Bathsheba. Her husband is the poor man. But have you ever thought about who the traveler is in Nathan's story? Who or what motivated David's decision? The traveler represents a lustful thought. You can't stop a traveler from coming through, but you don't have to take him in.

It's one thing to be tempted. We all are tempted in our own ways. Temptation isn't the sin. The thought that enters your mind isn't the sin. It's what you do with the thought that matters. When we let our lustful thoughts dominate our mind, well, that's going to be all we can think about. And that's just a little step away from acting on that kind of thought and inviting sin into your life. Now, the lamb was precious to the poor man. It was all he had. It was everything to him. And because the rich man took in the traveler, the lamb died. When you take in and feed on lustful imaginations and thoughts, something precious is going to die in your life. It could be your marriage. It could be someone else's. It could be the reputation you have. It could be joy and purpose. It might be the anointing.

Beware the traveler. The sins of lust start with a passing thought. This manifestation of the spirit of Jezebel is moving through the world in search of men or women who will let it in. And if that spirit is welcomed in with a hot meal and a warm bed, it will bring destruction on you.

Lustful sin is tempting for good reason. It can be pleasurable. Sometimes Christians act as if those who sin are having the worst time in the world. Well, maybe eventually it gets worse. But it feels good for a season. Even Paul wrote in Hebrews 11:25 about "the passing pleasures of sin." It's here, it may feel good, but then it's over, and so is the good feeling. And usually, the consequences roll in as painful aftershocks.

There are a few things we can learn from David and the "traveler":

1. *Stop at the one look.* David couldn't help what he saw, the image of a beautiful woman bathing, but he could choose how he responded to it. He could have gotten out his scrolls and read some Scripture, or gotten out his harp and sung a worship song, or done anything to get his mind back where it should have been. Instead, he did two things he shouldn't have done: He invited the thought to come in and visit, and he kept thinking about the woman. He asked around to find out who she was. He learned that her name was Bathsheba and that she was married to Uriah. And it didn't stop there. He fed the "traveler." He sent a messenger to have Bathsheba brought to him. That act eventually led to David's sin. It all began with an evil thought that David didn't control. He never guessed how far the traveler would take him. He became a liar, an adulterer and a murderer.

If you look long enough, your body is going to follow. We can't always help what we see in passing, but we can control our response. Often, the best thing we can do is what the Bible teaches, and what we saw Joseph do: Flee—take off in the opposite direction!

There's only one time we can find in the Bible where Christians are told to run away. First Corinthians 6:18 tells us, "Flee sexual immorality." Run—run away as fast as you can! The longer you stay on the computer, on the phone, in a conversation, out having a drink, in the same room, anywhere with someone you shouldn't be with or doing something you know you shouldn't be doing, leave. Go. Run. Now.

The longer you stay in a tempting situation, the weaker you will get.

2. *Don't be where you're not supposed to be.* The story of David and Bathsheba begins with this verse: "In the spring, at the time when kings go off to war, David sent Joab out with the king's men and the whole Israelite army" (2 Samuel 11:1 NIV). When kings were supposed to be out on the battlefield with the rest of their army, David stayed home. He was at the wrong place at the wrong time. Most people fall into temptation when they're in places they shouldn't be in or with people they're not supposed to be with. Where are you supposed to be? Check your location and make sure you're in the place where God wants you. If you're shirking responsibility or avoiding the hard work you know you've got to do, you'll be more likely to run into a traveler, as David did.

3. *Don't ask around about anybody or anything that presents a temptation.* After David looked and kept looking at Bathsheba, he asked his servants to find out about her. But why would a married man inquire about another woman? It was none of his business. We don't need to be asking around, searching on our computers, googling exes. This leaves us vulnerable. Stop asking around, whether asking other people or Google.

> To maintain sexual integrity, set and maintain your boundaries.

Your destination determines the route you take. To maintain sexual integrity, set and maintain your boundaries. Refuse to put yourself in a situation where you will be led into temptation. It's going to happen. No one is immune. So why choose to be at the wrong place at the wrong time when that dangerous next step can lead to death? Stay on guard. When the traveler knocks on your door, tell him to keep on traveling.

Wise Choices in the Worst of Times

Seldom do we get to make hard life choices in ideal circumstances. Have you noticed that when you are forced to make a decision, it happens under stress? And in that moment, you need to have something in you that is grounded, to keep you from throwing your life away on one crazy decision. I've seen great remorse on the face of many a husband who had that one-night stand after a fight with his wife. Why did he make such a terrible choice? He was angry and impulsive.

Emotions are often the culprits behind our bad decisions. Unless you decide beforehand what to do in certain circumstances, you are just a step away from making the wrong choice. This is why we are told to make a will or think about end-of-life decisions prior to being in those situations. If you don't decide what to do before the worst of times, you won't choose what's right during those worst times.

In Colossians 1:23, Paul talks about appearing irreproachable in God's sight by being "grounded and steadfast." The King James Version uses the words *grounded* and *settled*. The truth of your faith has to be settled, fixed and established as permanent in your mind before you get into a crisis or face a temptation. That's the only way you can make the best choices under less than perfect conditions.

It's like having a shopping list when you go to the store. If you walk through the doors of Target and stick with the items on your list, you'll walk out a few minutes later on target (pun unintended) with your plan and your budget. Take a trip to the store without having settled on what you're getting, and you'll be rolling out a cart bursting with bags full of stuff you don't need, and hundreds of dollars will have left your bank account. Settle your situation before it starts.

If you want to make good choices in the worst of circumstances, here are a few steps to take now to avoid sexual immorality later:

1. *Recognize you're vulnerable*. None of us, no matter our position or our platform, is immune to committing sexual immorality. One of the worst attitudes we can have is believing, *That can never happen to me*. It's not that we ought to guard our steps to the point of being paranoid about every move we or others make, but we should have a healthy recognition that no one is sin free.

2. *Maintain proper boundaries*. Pay attention to what you watch, what you listen to, whom you hang out with, places you go, things you do. Do any of these lead you down the road of temptation? Are you in a place that soon enough will be much harder to get out of? If you continue watching or listening or hanging out, will the taste start to sour?

It's important to preset limits on your personal space. Sometimes it's not the best idea to get too up-close and personal with someone of the opposite sex. A hug can linger too long. A touch can open doors that need to stay shut. Pay attention to the time you spend with someone. Is anything you're doing (like having your ego stroked, for example) creating an atmosphere that, although it's beginning to feel good, will surely lead down a slippery slope of destruction?

Finally, watch your body language. You can say a lot without saying a word.

3. *Seek help; reach out*. I read a story in a magazine about a married pastor who was attracted to a woman in his church. She was

attracted to him, too, though nothing physical or even emotional had happened. They'd just had a few conversations where the chemistry was obvious. He knew that further interactions with her wouldn't be wise. He also knew that seasons of temptation pass. He decided to connect with a friend he trusted. He told his pal, "If you're my true friend, I don't want you to ask me why, but I do want you for the next few weeks to call me at 6:00 p.m. every evening and ask me what I did all day."

The pastor's friend seemed confused, but he agreed to do it. Once three weeks passed, the pastor got his heart and mind in the right place, settled his boundaries and made up his mind to steer clear of this woman. This man made the wise choice by reaching out to his friend and choosing to be accountable to him, even if he didn't tell his buddy everything about the situation. It worked. It kept him in a lane of correct thinking and dampened a desire that would ultimately have cost both parties, and more, something precious.

We have a relentless enemy. You may think you've subdued sin today, but you must never forget that the devil is going to come back. If not tomorrow, he will return at another opportune time (see Luke 4:13).

Remember, Hair Always Grows Back

Certain things come to us as a shock, like a breakup or a sudden change in the weather. But there are some things that surprise us that really shouldn't be so unexpected. Like a car that runs out of gas when it's been on *E* all week, or a haircut that needs a trim in six to eight weeks.

You probably know the Bible story of Samson, the strongest man in Israel. He gave up the secret to his strength—his uncut hair—to a Philistine woman he was enamored of. She took a pair of scissors to his flowing mane and destroyed the man's life as he knew it. You can read the story in Judges 16. I want to look at Samson's story, but not from the perspective you might think. I won't dive into the dangers of temptations; we've already talked about that. I want us to look at it from the Philistines' perspective, specifically what they should have expected, but missed.

After Delilah had cut off Samson's hair, the Philistines captured him, blinded him, bound him in iron chains and put him to work in prison as a grinder. Here's the verse I find fascinating: "However, the hair of his head began to grow again after it had been shaven" (Judges 16:22).

That should have not been a surprise to anyone. There's nothing supernatural about hair growing back. You cut it, give it a few weeks' time, and it'll start to come in again. But I wonder why the Philistines, or whatever commander or general who led the kidnapping team, had not considered that a possibility. I mean, Samson wasn't your average tough man. He wasn't just a Navy SEAL operative; he was like a few elite special operations teams rolled into one man. He could kill a thousand soldiers on his own. He was strong, smart, savvy, resourceful, and most of all, he had the anointing of God on his life.

When Samson's scalp was bald, he was as intimidating as a toy poodle. I imagine within the first few days of his capture, the Philistines were on high alert, posting armed guards to watch Samson 24 hours a day, keeping his hands and feet shackled. But after a while, when the truth began to sink in that this strong man really had lost his strength, I imagine everyone began to relax around Samson. Maybe some even inched closer instead of keeping their distance. Maybe some people threw things at him, like spoiled food, or even slapped him upside the head. After all, Samson couldn't see what anyone was doing or what they were throwing. At some point, nobody was worried about Samson. He was no longer a threat.

The Philistines forgot the power that Samson had exhibited. Once his power was gone, they assumed it was gone forever. We do the same thing, don't we? We tend to forget that old habits and sins we conquered before do try to make a comeback. It can be a subtle comeback. Hair grows about half an inch a month, or half a millimeter a day. We're not usually re-tempted in a full-blown way after overcoming a previous temptation. It's a gradual letting down of the guard. In Samson's case, the guards who once watched him at all hours of the day and night were relieved of their duty. We might loosen our boundaries. Decide we don't need to be so militant. Perhaps our first look lingers. Or we show up somewhere we know we shouldn't be, but only for a few minutes. Don't be fooled. Hair grows back. Sometimes even stronger.

In Samson's final moments, a child led him into a great party the Philistines were throwing to celebrate their god, Dagon. Samson asked to be positioned in the center of the party, between the two middle pillars that supported the temple. The people wanted him to entertain them as they ate and drank and partied merrily. But Samson had other ideas:

> Then Samson said to the lad who held him by the hand, "Let me feel the pillars which support the temple, so that I can lean on them." Now the temple was full of men and women. All the lords of the Philistines were there—about three thousand men and women on the roof watching while Samson performed.
>
> Then Samson called to the LORD, saying, "O LORD God, remember me, I pray! Strengthen me, I pray, just this once, O God, that I may with one blow take vengeance on the Philistines for my two eyes!" And Samson took hold of the two middle pillars which supported the temple, and he braced himself against them, one on his right and the other on his left. Then Samson said, "Let me die with the Philistines!" And he pushed with all his might, and the temple fell on the lords and all the people who were in it. So the dead that he killed at his death were more than he had killed in his life.
>
> Judges 16:26–30

Any works of the enemy we allow to come back will come back stronger. We need to buzz cut sin. Keep it in its place. Away from our lives. When you open the door just a little, when you forget sin's strength, you will be at its mercy. And when an enemy is allowed to come back after you've kicked it out, well, it'll come back stronger. When Samson made a comeback, he wasn't weaker than before he had a forced haircut. He was stronger. He literally brought the entire house down and killed more in his death than in his entire life.

Jesus Himself taught this lesson about strong comebacks. He said,

> When an unclean spirit goes out of a man, he goes through dry places, seeking rest, and finds none. Then he says, "I will return to my house from which I came." And when he comes, he finds it empty, swept, and put in order. Then he goes and takes with him seven other spirits more wicked than himself, and they enter and dwell there; and the last state of that man is worse than the first. So shall it also be with this wicked generation.
>
> Matthew 12:43–45

That addiction you've overcome? Stay on guard. The porn you haven't watched in two weeks, that you're confident you're never going to look at again? Keep your boundaries in place. The affair you ended? Delete the number and forget his or her name. Take an aggressive stand against sin and keep your guard up.

The Spirit gives us desires that are opposite what the sinful nature desires. These two forces are constantly fighting against each other as we struggle to carry out our best intentions. Galatians 5:16–18 puts it this way:

> Walk in the Spirit, and you shall not fulfill the lust of the flesh. For the flesh lusts against the Spirit, and the Spirit against the flesh; and

these are contrary to one another, so that you do not do the things that you wish. But if you are led by the Spirit, you are not under the law.

It's a struggle as old as time itself. You must set biblical boundaries. Keep your mind, body, eyes, ears and behavior under the authority of the Holy Spirit.

You know who wins the battle between flesh and spirit? The one you feed the most. If you feed your carnal nature on impure thoughts, your flesh will win. On the other hand, if you feed the new nature you've been given on the Word of God, uplifting messages and wholesome thoughts, then your new nature will defeat the power of temptation to sin (see Philippians 4:8).

Sin is here to stay, but so is Jesus Christ. And through Him, God does not see you as being overcome by the lusts of the flesh. He sees you as an overcomer.

13

Living on the Edge of Eternity

I n November 1963, a famous playwright named David Lodge was sitting in Birmingham Repertory Theatre in England, watching his play "Between These Four Walls" being performed on stage. In the first act, one of the actors was supposed to turn on a radio and let it play. The audience was captivated by the actors and completely caught up in the play's entertainment, when suddenly a loud voice boomed over the radio, "Today, on November 22, 1963, in Dallas, Texas, President John F. Kennedy was shot and killed."

Everyone in the room was instantly stunned. The actor turned off the radio as quickly as he could, trying to save the rest of the performance. But it was too late. One by one, people began to leave the theatre. What was happening in the real world had ended the play world. The play was over! The hour of tragedy had struck, and the people were awakened.

Are you in a similar situation today? Is it possible that you have become so comfortable with everyday life that you have fallen asleep to the spiritual reality of what is truly happening? Playtime is over. It's time to wake up and realize that Jesus is coming soon.

196

And do this, knowing the time, that now it is high time to awake out of sleep; for now our salvation is nearer than when we first believed. The night is far spent, the day is at hand. Therefore let us cast off the works of darkness, and let us put on the armor of light. Let us walk properly, as in the day, not in revelry and drunkenness, not in lewdness and lust, not in strife and envy. But put on the Lord Jesus Christ, and make no provision for the flesh, to fulfill its lusts.

Romans 13:11–14

Some people have the idea that certain prophecies must be fulfilled before Jesus can come again. That's no longer true, because they now have been fulfilled. At any moment, Jesus might come.

We are living on the edge of eternity.

Occupy Until I Come

While we need to believe fully in the imminent return of Jesus Christ, we need to do more than just believe. We need to act, or in the words of Jesus, "occupy until I come" (Luke 19:13 KJV). One concept cannot outweigh the other.

We aren't supposed to just stick our heads in the sand while we await Christ's return. We shouldn't question whether we should continue to have families, or put into place a twenty-year plan for our future or make plans for next month. We occupy.

What does this mean? We dream and believe. Love and give. Serve and share. While we occupy this earth until Jesus returns, we must have a vision for the future.

Instead of giving up on people, or casting judgment, or hiding in a bunker or being seduced by end-time euphoria, we must pick up the weapons of the past: prayer, Bible reading and fasting. We need to act. We need to find the courage to stand up in this moment. We need to clean house and prepare our hearts.

The future is charged with enormous opportunity. Acts 2:17 tells us what we can expect:

> And it shall come to pass in the last days, says God, that I will pour out of My Spirit on all flesh; your sons and your daughters shall prophesy, your young men shall see visions, your old men shall dream dreams.

The chaos of our current events creates an open space for a generation of talented, innovative, forward-thinking people to step into politics, entertainment, media, academia, technology, business, medicine, law, entrepreneurship and science. To offset the doomsdaysayers, what if God plans to expand the role of our nations through the Church? I don't think He's through with any of us. I don't think it's over. We must challenge each other, and especially our young people. Are we teaching them how to discover God's vision for their lives? Are we showing the next generation why they are here, who they are and that whatever they do for God matters?

What we do on this earth for God matters. Acts 2:17 speaks of promised momentum. There's no passivity there. It's not the time to curl up in a fetal position and hide until Jesus appears for the second time. On the contrary—it's time to occupy by getting in the race to win.

Born to Win

In Genesis 49:19, a dying Jacob offered an unusual prophecy over Gad, one of his twelve sons: "Gad, a troop shall tramp upon him, but he shall triumph at last." Jacob told Gad that he would have a season when he felt as if he were losing, but in the end, when it mattered most, he would triumph. Gad was born to win, not to lose.

What a powerful prophecy. When he was born, his mother named him Gad, which means "a troop cometh." In other words, she saw the negative forces he would have to face. But Jacob saw it differently.

Like Gad, I know there will be times in your life when you feel trampled. But I'm telling you, that is not your destiny. You were not born to lose. You were not born to be insignificant. And so, when you have times when it looks as if you're losing, you have to remind yourself who your God is and what He says about you. In the end, you were born to win.

There will be times when it feels as if you can't put one foot in front of the other. Your dreams may be smashed. You will feel as though you're being trampled to the ground. But God said that you were not born to be defeated. You were not born to chase after trivial things. Again, you were not born to lose. In these times of uncertainty, remember Whose you are. God has a powerful destiny for your life.

First John 4:4 puts it like this: "You are of God, little children, and have overcome them, because He who is in you is greater than he who is in the world." You are born of God, and He is calling you to higher things. So while you may encounter problems, you are an overcomer—that's part of your identity. You may experience another pandemic, more global conflicts and deeper political divide,

> **While you may encounter problems, you are an overcomer— that's part of your identity.**

but what God put in you is stronger than the events of the day. You are going to the other side. You were not born to quit. God did not bring you this far so you could end up in a could have/should have/ would have story.

The Word of God says you are the head and not the tail. You are above only and not beneath (see Deuteronomy 28:13). You are a world shaker and a devil disturber. Wake up the giant that is inside you. Remember the words of Jesus: "I will build My church, and the gates of Hades shall not prevail against it" (Matthew 16:18). You are the house of God. He didn't make you His house, only to move away in the bad times.

Right now, you may not feel as though you are winning. But like Gad, if you will grab hold of God's promises, you will be victorious in the end.

You were born to win.

Tips to Win the Spiritual Olympics

The apostle Paul lived during the time of the ancient Olympics. The first games date back to 776 BC and consisted of a one-day event. In 684 BC, the games were extended to last three days. In the fifth century BC, the Olympic Games covered five days and included running, long jump, shot put, javelin, boxing, pankration and equestrian events.[1] Women were not allowed to compete; they would eventually have separate games of their own. It may have had something to do with the fact that many of the male contestants competed naked (clothes were said to have impeded endurance, stamina and speed).

Unlike today, the wrestling and pankration (a mix of boxing and wrestling) events had few rules—mainly no biting or gouging. One grueling event was the hoplite race. Competitors were required to run either 384 meters or 768 meters while wearing standard hoplite armor that weighed about fifty pounds. Finally, winners of the Olympics received not gold medals, but crowns made of olive leaves taken from a wild and sacred olive tree near the Temple of Zeus. Back then, it was believed that whoever wore those particular leaves acquired divine qualities like the god Zeus. The lucky victors also had a statue erected in their honor in their hometown.

If you look closely, you'll notice that some of the letters Paul wrote to the Church were peppered with competitive language, as if he is comparing the journey of faith to the Olympic Games. Take the following Scriptures:

> Do you not know that those who run in a race all run, but one receives the prize? Run in such a way that you may obtain it (1 Corinthians 9:24).

> I have fought the good fight, I have finished the race, I have kept the faith (2 Timothy 4:7).

I love the imagery Paul uses in Hebrews 12:1–2:

> Therefore we also, since we are surrounded by so great a cloud of witnesses, let us lay aside every weight, and the sin which so easily ensnares us, and let us run with endurance the race that is set before us, looking unto Jesus, the author and finisher of our faith, who for the joy that was set before Him endured the cross, despising the shame, and has sat down at the right hand of the throne of God.

I think of this passage as Paul's pep talk to Christians as we engage in our own spiritual Olympics. Untie what holds you back, run with endurance, keep your eyes set on Jesus. This is great coaching for us today. As you find yourself scrolling through negative feeds that paint the devastating picture of systemic racism, the removal of religion from society, hatred spewing on all sides, legislation after legislation passed not in alignment with the Word of God, I want to offer you five tips on what it means to occupy on this earth, to wait with anticipation for Christ's return and also to engage in the race of life.

Tip #1: Strive to master.

Ecclesiastes 9:10 (NASB) gives us solid advice: "Whatever your hand finds to do, do it with all your might." Another way of putting it is, "Be the very best that you can be at whatever you do." If you teach, be the best. If you're an athlete, train to win. If you're a stay-at-home parent, give your all.

Traveling almost forty miles per hour, Olympic divers enter the water from a ten-meter (3.3 story) platform. If the divers don't hit the water just right, the impact is enough to break their wrists. It's one reason you probably see divers' wrists all taped up when they're competing. In addition to hours of dry land training, these competitors practice in the pool daily for three to six hours. They know how to get in the training they need to master their craft. Like those divers, we need a spiritual attitude that says, "I'm striving to be the best."

Tip #2: Strive to win.

Live with a winner's mentality. During ancient times, only one winner in each event was awarded the prize. There were no gold, silver or bronze medals. You either won and collected a crown, or you didn't. When it comes to our spiritual lives, I wonder how often we settle for second best. We resign ourselves to a bad habit. We accept cheap substitutes for the abundant life Jesus came to give us.

I wonder if Paul had the imagery of the Olympic Games in mind when he penned these words: "Do you not know that those who run in a race all run, but one receives the prize? Run in such a way that you may obtain it" (1 Corinthians 9:24). Get in it to win it!

We must not be comfortable with less than winning. Put your heart and soul into the dreams God has called you to achieve, the goals He has equipped you to reach and the lives He has entrusted you to reach. There's no trophy for participation here. Either you win or you don't. Go for the gold!

Tip #3: Take responsibility for your effort.

There were no team events in the ancient Olympic Games. Everyone competed on an individual level. Likewise now in your spiritual race, even if your parents went to church or your grand-mother was a prayer warrior, their legacies don't just become your achievements. Paul wrote, "So then each of us shall give account of himself to God" (Romans 14:12). When you stand before the throne on Judgment Day, you're going to have to speak on behalf of yourself for what you've done with your life. Did you give to the poor? Did you lend mercy? Were you willing to pick up the phone when somebody on the other end needed prayer? Were you an asset to the ministry of the Lord Jesus Christ, or did you just show up?

Tip #4: Never quit.

The winners of games—and of life— are those who don't give up. Athletes who wanted to compete in the ancient Olympics were required to take an oath saying they had trained in their event for ten months prior to the games. Thirty days prior to the games, they gathered for preliminary training and were judged to see who would participate in the actual games. Once they were assigned as participants, they could not quit. May we all live in such a way that when we meet Jesus, we can say, "I have fought the good fight, I have finished the race, I have kept the faith" (2 Timothy 4:7). Press through. Remain faithful. Don't give up.

Three days before he was supposed to compete in the 1976 Olympics, a boxer named Howard David lost his mother to a heart attack. He was crushed. His first instinct told him to go home. But instead, he decided to win a gold medal for her. He said, "I was willing to die before losing. I was going to leave it all in the ring."[2] Not only did Davis come home with a gold medal, but he was also awarded the Val Barker Trophy for being the best technical boxer, named over his legendary teammate Sugar Ray Leonard.

You will get knocked down. I will, too. But let's commit to get-ting up every time. Make up your mind not to quit. We will endure till the end.

Tip #5. Remember who is cheering for you.

When Paul encourages us to run the race with endurance in Hebrews 12, he talks about how "we are surrounded by so great a cloud of witnesses" (verse 1). I imagine he might have seen the crowds that packed the Olympic site, where thousands upon thousands of enthused voices were thundering with passion, pride and encouragement.

In our race of faith, we have the home court advantage. Right now in heaven there stands a cloud of witnesses, men and women who have passed on, like Abraham, Isaac, Ruth and Jacob. And every now and then, they are allowed to peek into our lives on earth and cheer us on from the grandstands of glory. They are telling you and me, "Don't quit. Don't stop. Don't give up." My grandfather is there, too. And my father, and my brother. I get encouraged when I think about them telling me, "Run! You're going to win if you won't quit!"

Being a Christian today doesn't warrant much encouragement from the world. Taking a stand for God, or choosing His standards over our culture's priorities, will not prompt applause here on earth. But remember, even though we're not in their presence yet, we have a cloud of witnesses jumping out of their seats and screaming at the top of their lungs, "Run the race! Win the medal! Go for the gold!"

Here's the best part of all: Jesus is standing at our finish line. Look again at the final part of Hebrews 12:1–2:

> Let us run with endurance the race that is set before us, looking unto Jesus, the author and finisher of our faith, who for the joy that was set before Him endured the cross, despising the shame, and has sat down at the right hand of the throne of God.

"We must all appear before the judgment seat of Christ," 2 Corinthians 5:10 tells us. The Greek word used for judgment here is *bema*, which means "of the official seat of a judge . . . of the judgment seat of Christ."[3] I like to think of this judgment seat as an award stand, like the kind in the Olympics where they give out the crowns or medals.

One day, you are going to stand before the judgment seat. What will you have to say for yourself? What investments will you have to show? What legacy will you tell God that you left behind? What souls can you point to whom you have led to Christ?

I am not writing these words in judgment. I am preparing you for what's to come and prompting you, in love, to stop and think. Are you ready? Is your house in order? Have you done all that God has asked of you? Are you using or burying your talent?

It's time to stop settling for second best and get your eyes on the eternal prize. Instead of being fearful of or paralyzed by the knowledge of what will happen in the last days, remember that God is preparing you for this. Now is not the time to slow down, but the time to continue enduring and aim for the prize.

A Jehu Generation

While Satan, through many means including the spirit of Jezebel, toils day and night to destroy the Kingdom of God, know that God has a turnaround anointing in store for His people that will destroy the enemy.

In 1 Kings 19:15–16, God told the prophet Elijah to anoint a commander of chariots under King Ahab by the name of Jehu, and also to name his successor, Elisha, as the next prophet. When Elisha took Elijah's place, he directed one of the prophets on his team to anoint Jehu as the king of Israel and prophesy that he would destroy Jezebel and all of Ahab's house (see 2 Kings 9:1–10).

At that time, the nation of Israel was divided into two kingdoms, the Northern Kingdom of Judah and the Southern Kingdom of Israel. Joram, a terribly evil king, reigned over the Southern Kingdom. He also happened to be the son of King Ahab and Queen Jezebel.

Joram's nephew, Ahaziah, ruled over the Northern Kingdom of Judah. God had a plan for Jehu to decimate the dynasty of Ahab and Jezebel. Jehu was anointed under these words:

> Thus says the LORD God of Israel: "I have anointed you king over the people of the LORD, over Israel. You shall strike down the house of Ahab your master, that I may avenge the blood of My servants the prophets, and the blood of all the servants of the LORD, at the hand of Jezebel. For the whole house of Ahab shall perish; and I will cut off from Ahab all the males in Israel, both bond and free. So I will make the house of Ahab like the house of Jeroboam the son of Nebat, and like the house of Baasha the son of Ahijah. The dogs shall eat Jezebel on the plot of ground at Jezreel, and there shall be none to bury her."
>
> 2 Kings 9:6–10

The anointing to be king was a big deal. Now, when you think of an anointing by oil, you may picture a prophet dabbing Jehu on the forehead with an oil-smeared finger. But at the time, it was much more dramatic. The book of Exodus tells us that the anointing oil used for this was equal to about six quarts, or roughly a gallon and a half. Jehu was soaked in oil!

When Jehu calmly told the men what God had told him, that he was going to become the next king, they went crazy. They grabbed trumpets and started blowing them and saying, "Jehu, he is king! Jehu, he is king!" And then they took their coats off, because if he's a king, he needs a throne. And the Bible said that there was a staircase near them, so they threw their coats down on the steps, and they led him up the steps, and then made a pile with their coats and told him to sit on it because he was the king!

So here sits Jehu, an ordinary if oily man, on top of a heap of worn coats. But what he had was more than enough—he had the anointing of God. And that anointing was going to turn around the nation of Israel from a state of wickedness to one of righteousness.

Jehu hopped on his horse and furiously rode to the palace to share the news, knowing the kings in charge were not going to be impressed or so easily set aside their reign. King Joram was convalescing from some battle wounds, and was being visited by King Ahaziah, with whom he had formed an alliance. When Jehu got close, a messenger ran from the palace to greet him and ask if he came in peace.

"What have you to do with peace?" Jehu replied. "Turn around and follow me" (2 Kings 9:18). The messenger did so, obviously struck by the anointing Jehu had just received from God. The guy turned his horse around and started riding with the army of the Lord! The same thing happened again, with a second messenger. *Wop*, it hit him, too!

Finally, both kings headed out of the palace on their chariots to meet Jehu. Jehu shot King Joram between the arms and he fell in his chariot, dead. Seeing what just happened, King Ahaziah took off, running for his life. Jehu pursued him and had him killed, too.

Jezebel, who was in the palace, got wind of what had gone down. When she heard that Jehu was gunning for her, she resorted to her seductive and manipulative tactics. She got all dolled up—makeup, hair and bling. Can you picture her caking on her foundation while batting her eyelashes, whispering to herself, *Jehu may have killed those kings, but he hasn't dealt with me yet.* . . . When Jezebel was done blotting the shine on her forehead, she poked her head out the window of her room.

Jehu rode up, looked up at the window and said, "Who is on my side? Who?" (2 Kings 9:32). Two or three eunuchs looked out to him. "Throw her down," Jehu commanded them (verse 33).

The men grabbed Jezebel and hurled her out the window. Bones crunched and blood splattered. A horse trampled over her dead body. When it came time to bury her, all that could be found were her skull, her feet and the palms of her hands. Wild dogs had eaten the rest. This was fulfillment of the prophetic anointing spoken over Jehu.

Satan is trying hard to convince you to give up. To turn you around from a committed marriage, a precious family, a great opportunity down the road, a life of purpose. But when the enemy comes in like a flood, the Spirit of the Lord will lift up a standard against him (see Isaiah 59:19). God is anointing a Jehu generation to stand up and fight for Him. You and I are among them.

Yes, we are living on the edge of eternity. This is our finest hour as believers! I believe God wants the Church to get so anointed that we begin to understand that our point in being here is to turn this thing around.

We've talked a lot about the ancient spirit of Jezebel. Now I want to show you a modern example of how that spirit remains with us. Madalyn Murray O'Hair, a denier of the Holocaust, was the founder of the American Atheists organization and served as its president from 1963–1986. One of her sons, Jon Garth, became its president from 1986–1995, although it was still Madalyn herself who wielded true control over the organization. She also founded the *American Atheist Magazine*.

Yes, we are living on the edge of eternity. This is our finest hour as believers!

O'Hair filed several lawsuits that dealt with First Amendment separation of church and state issues. She is best known for *Murray v. Curtlett*, in which she challenged a 1905 Baltimore school board rule requiring that the school day began with either a reading from the Bible or the Lord's Prayer. The case, consolidated with a similar case (*Abington School District v. Schempp*), went before the Supreme Court in 1963. The court ruled that both Bible reading and the Lord's Prayer, as well as public school–sponsored religious activities, violated the Constitution.

O'Hair didn't stop at removing the Bible from school. She sought to remove the phrase "In God We Trust" from American currency and outlaw tax exemptions for churches and clergy. She also sued the Pope. All those lawsuits failed. In 1964, *LIFE* magazine called her "the most hated woman in America," a label she took great pleasure in owning. She spent most of her life advocating for the removal of religion.

The success of her organization began to dwindle, however, as she began to alienate its members. Before long, she had no friends and socialized only with her son Jon Garth, and her granddaughter, Robin, working and living exclusively with the two of them. O'Hair's health began to decline rapidly. She suffered from diabetes, high blood pressure and dizziness, and could walk only with the assistance of a walker or wheelchair.

In 1995, O'Hair, Robin and Jon Garth suddenly disappeared from Austin, Texas. Word on the street was that they probably vanished to New Zealand due to rising financial and legal woes. Five years later, the trio was found. Investigations revealed that they were kidnapped by three men, one of whom worked for the American Atheists organization as an office manager. The men extorted over half a million dollars from O'Hair before they killed her, along with her son and granddaughter.

The life and death of Madalyn O'Hair parallel that of the Old Testament's Queen Jezebel in a number of ways. Both women were a controversy in their nation and were unpopular among the righteous. Both women's influence continued on even after their death. Yet the story isn't over. Although the Supreme Court hasn't yet overturned the case O'Hair won, one of her children is still fighting the same battle his mother fought. But unlike her, today he is battling on the Lord's side. By 1980, O'Hair's first son, William J. Murray, was a struggling alcoholic. One night, he had a dream. It ended with an angel who carried a giant sword, the tip of which touched an open

Bible. Murray's life was changed forever after that dream. He became a Christian—the antithesis of everything his mother had fought for. In his words, "It wasn't a reaction to my mother's atheism. It was a reaction to the chaos I was subjected to for the first eighteen years of my life. That I was able to survive at all proves there is a God."[4] A minister and bestselling author, Murray presently (as of this writing) chairs the Religious Freedom Coalition. One of its main goals is to restore prayer in schools.

Time to Fly

Know this: While the spirit of Jezebel is active, mighty and seeking to destroy, the legacy she leaves is not one you are destined to carry. You may feel overwhelmed in this very moment, but God has created you to overcome! No matter what your background or what addictions lie in your genetics, the spirit of God is exceedingly and abundantly able, and willing, to fulfill His purposes in your life. You just have to say yes.

God is stirring up your nest for a reason. The stress, troubles and trials are not meant to overwhelm you to the point of giving up, although I know at times it feels that way. Think of what hurts as gentle nudges reminding you to fix your eyes toward the sky and start spreading your wings. Something greater is at work. What hurts today will one day, in the blink of an eye, vanish. And until then, God wants you to remember that you were born to fly.

God is breathing new life into your destiny. I can't tell you what the future holds for your life. I can't tell you what tomorrow holds for the world. But I know a day is coming when Jesus will return, and until that day comes, He has a plan for your life, a purpose that is unfolding right now.

Paul Rader, an evangelist who has already gone to heaven, used to say, "We are living so close to the second coming of Jesus Christ that

I can hear the tinkling of the silverware as the angels are setting the table for the marriage supper of the Lamb."[5] This will be a glorious celebration at which all who are in Christ will honor Jesus and His rightful reign on this earth. It will be a reunion of the saints, past and present, to glorify the King of kings.

"Therefore you also be ready, for the Son of Man is coming at an hour you do not expect" (Matthew 24:44).

Are you ready?

A SPECIAL INVITATION

Once you have decided that you believe Jesus is the way to salvation and you call on Him for the forgiveness of your sins, nothing can separate you from His love. If you have read this book and have not yet made the decision to trust in Jesus, I'd like to invite you to pray a prayer of salvation right now:

Dear God, I am praying because I know I need a Savior. I believe that Jesus is the Son of God, and that He died for my sins and rose again on the third day. I am asking You to forgive my sins, and I believe that through Jesus, I am forgiven. Amen.

If you have just prayed this prayer, I'd love to hear from you. Share your story with us today at jentezenfranklin.org.

NOTES

Introduction

1. Bible Hub, s.v. "5467.chalepos," https://biblehub.com/greek/5467.htm.

2. William Stearns Davis, *Readings in Ancient History: Rome and the West* (Boston: Allyn and Bacon, 1913), 150, accessed at Google Books, https://books.google.com/books?vid=LCCN12017957.

Chapter 1 When You're Walking, God Is Working

1. Evan Andrews, "Did a Premature Obituary Inspire the Nobel Prize?," History.com, updated July 23, 2020, https://www.history.com/news/did-a-premature-obituary-inspire-the-nobel-prize.

2. Ibid.

3. Ibid.

Chapter 3 Step #1: Look Within

1. The Free Dictionary, s.v. "high-value target," https://www.thefreedictionary.com/high-value+target. See also *Dictionary of Military and Associated Terms*, s.v. "high-value target," U.S. Department of Defense, 2005.

2. Bible Tools: Greek/Hebrew Definitions, s.v. "shamar" (Strong's H8104), https://www.bibletools.org/index.cfm/fuseaction/Lexicon.show/ID/H8104/shamar.htm.

3. Ancient Hebrew Research Center, s.v. "keep/shamar" (Strong's H8104), https://www.ancient-hebrew.org/definition/keep.htm.

4. Bible Hub, s.v. "4625.skandalon," https://biblehub.com/greek/4625.htm.

5. Bible Hub, s.v. "3783.opheiléma," https://biblehub.com/greek/3783.htm.

6. Bible Tools: Greek/Hebrew Definitions, s.v. "hupomeno" (Strong's G5278), https://www.bibletools.org/index.cfm/fuseaction/Lexicon.show/ID/G5278/hupomeno.htm.

Chapter 4 Step #2: Look to Him

1. Tino Wallenda, "The Show Must Go On," *Victorious Living*, May 2019, https://victoriouslivingmagazine.com/2019/04/the-show-must-go-on/.

2. Dotty Brown, "'Row the Boat': A Philosophy for Living," Boathouse Row, August 19, 2019, https://boathouserowthebook.com/2019/08/19/row-the-boat-a-philosophy-for-living/.

3. Bible Study Tools, s.v. "peran" (Strong's G4008), https://www.biblestudytools.com/lexicons/greek/nas/peran.html.

Chapter 5 Step #3: Look Ahead

1. Shaun Jex, "Remembering Joe Fowler," *Celebrations* (blog), February 26, 2018, https://celebrationspress.com/2018/02/26/remembering-admiral-joe-fowler/.

2. Wolfgang Saxon, "Joseph Fowler, 99, Builder of Warships and Disney's Parks," *New York Times*, December 14, 1993, http://query.nytimes.com/gst/fullpage.html?.

3. For more on Joe Fowler, see Walt Disney Archives online, "Disney Legends: Joe Fowler," https://d23.com/walt-disney-legend/joe-fowler/.

4. Bible Hub, s.v. "7648.soba," https://biblehub.com/hebrew/7648.htm.

5. Jentezen Franklin, *Believe That You Can* (Lake Mary, Fla.: Charisma House, 2008), Kindle edition, chapter 2.

6. Dictionary.com, s.v. "conquer," https://www.dictionary.com/browse/conquer.

7. For more on Douglas Mackiernan's story, visit https://www.washingtonpost.com/wp-srv/national/longterm/ciamag/cia2.htm, and https://www.cia.gov/legacy/honoring-heroes/heroes/douglas-s-mackiernan/.

Chapter 6 Step #4: Look Out

1. Leah MarieAnn Klett, "Entire Bible translated into 700 languages; 5.7 billion people now have access to Scripture," *Christian Post*, October 6, 2020, https://www.christianpost.com/news/entire-bible-translated-into-700-languages.html.

2. Elbert Hubbard, *A Message to Garcia* (Mumbai, Maharashtra: Sanage Publishing, 2020), Kindle edition, page 8.

Chapter 7 Step #5: Look Up

1. Jonathan Snowden, "Muhammad Ali's Greatest Fight: George Foreman and the Rumble in the Jungle," Bleacher Report, June 4, 2016, https://bleacherreport.com/articles/1919959-muhammad-alis-greatest-fight-george-foreman-and-the-rumble-in-the-jungle.

2. Danielle De Wolfe, "George Foreman on why Muhammad Ali was so much more than a 'boxer,'" ShortList, June 4, 2016, https://www.shortlist.com/news/george-foreman-on-ali.

3. Casey Chan, "You Will Spend 43 Days on Hold in Your Life," Gizmodo, January 25, 2013, https://gizmodo.com/you-will-spend-43-days-on-hold-in-your-life-5979168.

4. AJ Willingham, "Commuters waste an average of 54 hours a year stalled in traffic, study says," CNN, updated August 22, 2019, https://www.cnn.com /2019/08/22/us/traffic-commute-gridlock-transportation-study-trnd/index.html.

5. John Tesh, "The average person will spend 10 years standing in line over their lifetime!," *Intelligence for Your Life*, https://www.tesh.com/articles/the-average -person-will-spend-10-years-standing-in-line-over-their-lifetime/.

6. "Brits Spend 6.7 Years of Their Lives Just Waiting Around," Direct Line Group, August 16, 2019, https://www.directlinegroup.co.uk/en/news/brand-news /2019/17082019.html.

Chapter 8 The Overwhelming

1. "One in 100 deaths is by suicide," World Health Organization, June 17, 2021, https://www.who.int/news/item/17-06-2021-one-in-100-deaths-is-by-suicide.

2. Ibid.

3. "Mental Health by the Numbers," National Alliance on Mental Illness (NAMI), last updated March 2021, https://www.nami.org/mhstats. See also "Anxiety Disorders," NAMI, last updated December 2017, https://www.nami.org/About -Mental-Illness/Mental-Health-Conditions/Anxiety-Disorders.

4. "Forced labour, modern slavery and human trafficking," International Labour Organization (ILO), https://www.ilo.org/global/topics/forced-labour/lang --en/index.htm.

Chapter 9 Face Fear with Faith

1. Bible Hub, s.v. "2350.thorubeo," https://biblehub.com/greek/2350.htm.

2. Natalie O'Neill, "Most searched phobia of 2020 is fear of other people, researchers say," Fox News, October 19, 2020, https://www.foxnews.com/lifestyle /phobia-2020-fear-other-people-google.

3. For more information on this, see Max Roser, Esteban Ortiz-Ospina, and Hannah Ritchie, "Life Expectancy," Our World in Data, last updated October 2019, https://ourworldindata.org/life-expectancy#life-expectancy-has-improved -globally.

Chapter 10 Dismantling Discouragement

1. "*It's a Wonderful Life* Beginning with Prayers and Angels Talking," YouTube, https://www.youtube.com/watch?v=79pIurpNARs.

2. Rhema Team, "The God Who Is More Than Enough," Rhema.org, June 8, 2020, https://events.rhema.org/the-god-who-is-more-than-enough/.

Chapter 11 Dig Out of Depression

1. Daniel G. Amen, M.D., "Do You Have an ANT Infestation in Your Head?," *Amen* Clinics, September 16, 2020, https://www.amenclinics.com/blog/do-you -have-an-ant-infestation-in-your-head/.

Chapter 12 Fight the Flesh

1. "Pornography Statistics," CovenantEyes, https://www.covenanteyes.com/pornstats/.

2. "Things Are Looking Up in American's Porn Industry," NBC News, January 20, 2015, https://www.nbcnews.com/business/business-news/things-are-looking-americas-porn-industry-n289431.

3. Paul J. Wright, Robert S. Tokunaga, and Ashley Kraus, "A Meta-Analysis of Pornography Consumption and Actual Acts of Sexual Aggression in General Population Studies," *Journal of Communication* 66, no. 1 (February 2016): 183–205.

4. Barna Group, "Porn in the Digital Age: New Research Reveals 10 Trends," April 6, 2016, https://www.barna.com/research/porn-in-the-digital-age-new-research-reveals-10-trends/.

5. "Pornography Statistics," CovenantEyes, https://www.covenanteyes.com/pornstats/.

6. Ibid.

7. Jane E. Brody, "Personal Health: When a Partner Cheats," *New York Times*, January 22, 2018, https://www.nytimes.com/2018/01/22/well/marriage-cheating-infidelity.html.

8. "Half of U.S. Christians say casual sex between consenting adults is sometimes or always acceptable," Pew Research Center, Washington, D.C. (August 31, 2020), https://www.pewresearch.org/fact-tank/2020/08/31/half-of-u-s-christians-say-casual-sex-between-consenting-adults-is-sometimes-or-always-acceptable/.

9. Dictionary.com, s.v. "incur," https://www.dictionary.com/browse/incur.

Chapter 13 Living on the Edge of Eternity

1. For more on the ancient Olympics, see "Welcome to the Ancient Olympic Games," International Olympic Committee, https://olympics.com/ioc/ancient-olympic-games.

2. Kyle Symes, "Olympic Gold Medalist Howard Davis Jr.: A Champion Inside and Outside the Ring," Bleacher Report, March 6, 2012, https://bleacherreport.com/articles/1092130-olympic-gold-medalist-howard-davis-jr-a-champion-in-and-out-of-the-ring.

3. Bible Study Tools, s.v. "bema," https://www.biblestudytools.com/lexicons/greek/nas/bema.html.

4. Michelle Bearden, "Confessions of an Unbeliever," *Tampa Bay Times*, October 16, 2005, https://www.tampabay.com/archive/1990/04/22/confessions-of-an-unbeliever/.

5. Adrian Rogers and Steve Rogers, *Unveiling the End Times in Our Time: The Triumph of the Lamb in Revelation* (Nashville: B&H Publishing Group, 2004, 2013), 220.

Jentezen Franklin is the senior pastor of Free Chapel, a multicampus church with a global reach. His messages influence generations through modern-day technology and digital media, his televised broadcast, *Kingdom Connection*, and outreaches that put God's love and compassion into action. Jentezen is also a *New York Times* bestselling author who speaks at conferences worldwide. He and his wife, Cherise, live in Gainesville, Georgia, and have five children and four grandchildren. Find out more at JentezenFranklin.org.

More Teaching from Jentezen Franklin

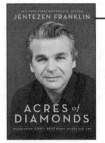
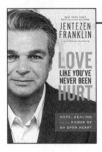